100 Songs in  **the Key of "C"**

THE EASY TWENTIES FAKE BOOK

ISBN 978-1-4234-6391-7

HAL•LEONARD®
CORPORATION
7777 W. Bluemound Rd. P.O. Box 13819 Milwaukee, WI 53213

THE EASY TWENTIES FAKE BOOK

CONTENTS

INTRODUCTION

What Is a Fake Book?

A fake book has one-line music notation consisting of melody, lyrics and chord symbols. This lead sheet format is a "musical shorthand" that is an invaluable resource for all musicians—hobbyists to professionals.

Here's how *The Easy Twenties Fake Book* differs from most standard fake books:

- All songs are in the key of C.

- Many of the melodies have been simplified.

- Only five basic chord types are used—major, minor, seventh, diminished and augmented.

- The music notation is larger for ease of reading.

In the event that you haven't used chord symbols to create accompaniment, or your experience is limited, a chord speller chart is included at the back of the book to help you get started.

Have fun!

AIN'T MISBEHAVIN'
from AIN'T MISBEHAVIN'

Words by ANDY RAZAF
Music by THOMAS "FATS" WALLER and HARRY BROOKS

AIN'T SHE SWEET

Words by JACK YELLEN
Music by MILTON AGER

Medium bright tempo

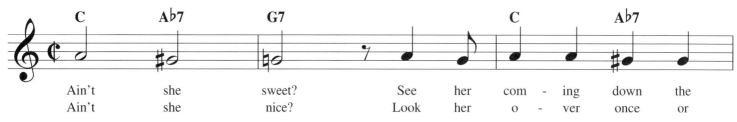

Ain't she sweet? See her com - ing down the
Ain't she nice? Look her o - ver once or

street. Now I ask you ver - y con - fi - den - tial - ly
twice. Now I ask you ver - y con - fi - den - tial - ly

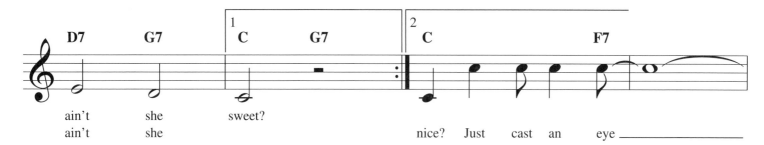

ain't she sweet?
ain't she nice? Just cast an eye _____

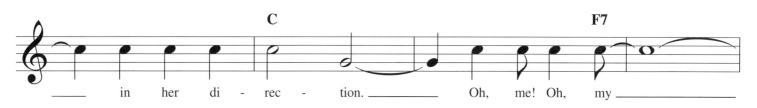

____ in her di - rec - tion. ____ Oh, me! Oh, my _____

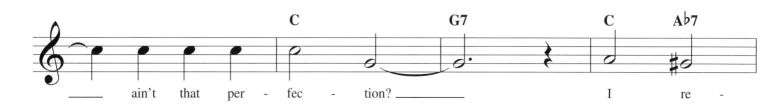

____ ain't that per - fec - tion? _____ I re -

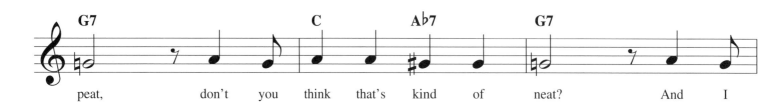

peat, don't you think that's kind of neat? And I

ask you ver - y con - fi - den - tial - ly ain't she sweet?

ALABAMY BOUND
from THE GREAT AMERICAN BROADCAST

Words by B.G. DeSYLVA and BUD GREEN
Music by RAY HENDERSON

ALL ALONE

Words and Music by
IRVING BERLIN

Moderately

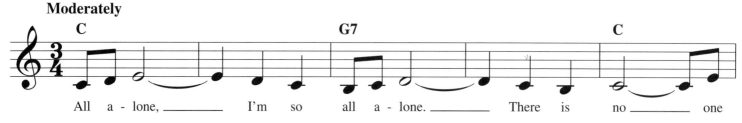

All a - lone, _____ I'm so all a - lone. _____ There is no _____ one

else _____ but you. _____ All a - lone _____ by the

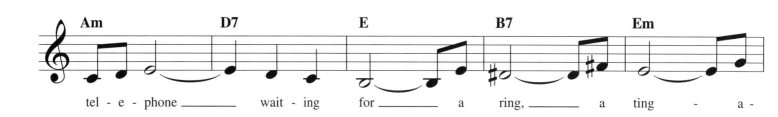

tel - e - phone _____ wait - ing for _____ a ring, _____ a ting - a -

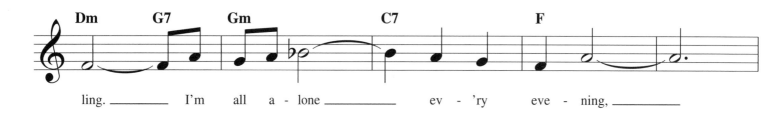

ling. _____ I'm all a - lone _____ ev - 'ry eve - ning, _____

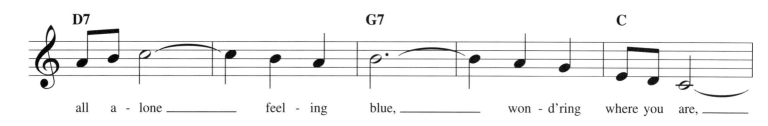

all a - lone _____ feel - ing blue, _____ won - d'ring where you are, _____

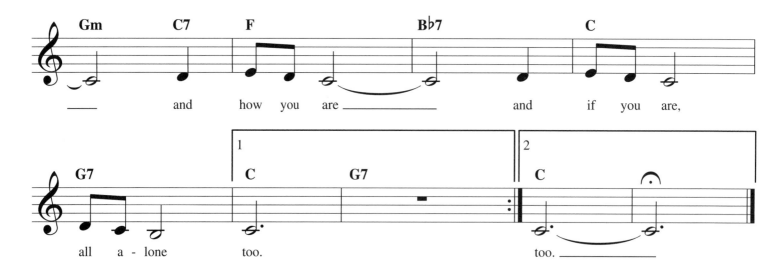

_____ and how you are _____ and if you are,

all a - lone too.

1. C   G7

2. C

too. _____

ALWAYS

Words and Music by
IRVING BERLIN

Moderate Waltz

I'll   be   lov-ing   you   al - ways, _____ with   a   love   that's

true   al - ways. _____ When   the things you've planned   need   a   help-ing

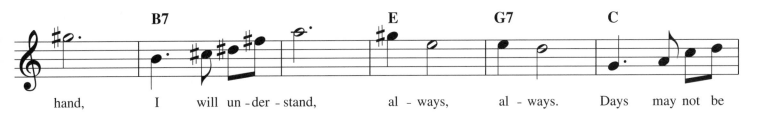

hand,   I   will un-der-stand,   al - ways,   al - ways.   Days   may not be

fair   al - ways. _____ That's   when I'll be   there,

al - ways, _____ not   for just an   hour,   not   for just a

day,   not   for just a   year,   but   al - ways. _____

AMAPOLA
(Pretty Little Poppy)

By JOSEPH M. LACALLE
New English Words by ALBERT GAMSE

ANGRY

Words by DUDLEY MECUM
Music by JULES CASSARD,
HENRY BRUNIES and MERRITT BRUNIES

AMONG MY SOUVENIRS

Words by EDGAR LESLIE
Music by HORATIO NICHOLLS

Slowly, with expression

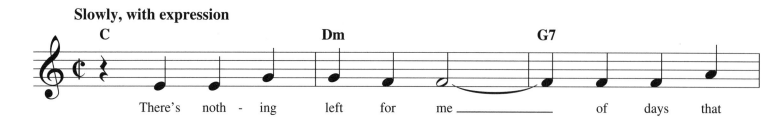

There's noth-ing left for me _____ of days that

used to be. _____ I live in mem-o-ry a-

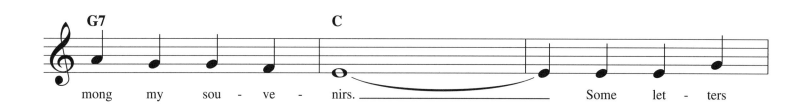

mong my sou-ve-nirs. _____ Some let-ters

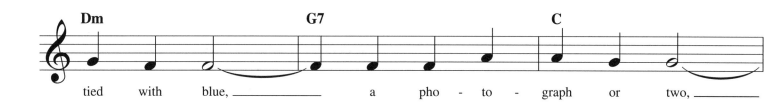

tied with blue, _____ a pho-to-graph or two, _____

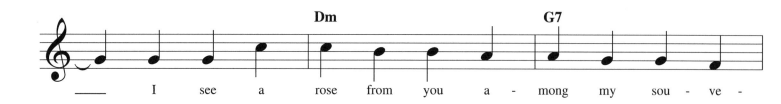

_____ I see a rose from you a-mong my sou-ve-

nirs. _____ A few more to - kens rest _____

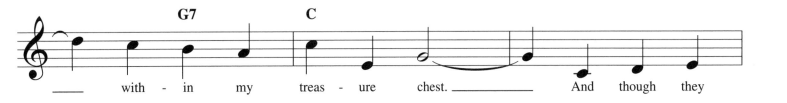

_____ with - in my treas - ure chest. _____ And though they

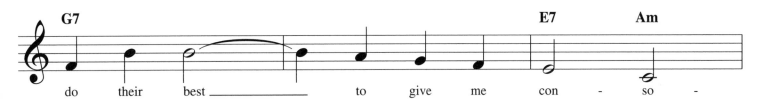

do their best _____ to give me con - so -

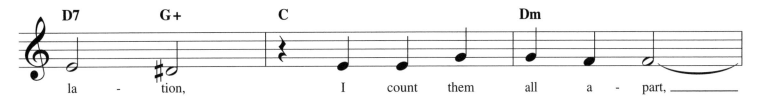

la - tion, I count them all a - part, _____

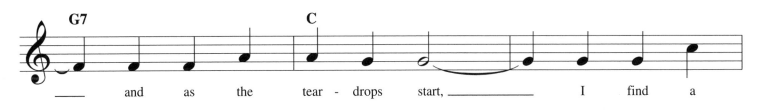

_____ and as the tear - drops start, _____ I find a

bro - ken heart a - mong my sou - ve - nirs. _____

AT SUNDOWN

Words and Music by
WALTER DONALDSON

Moderately

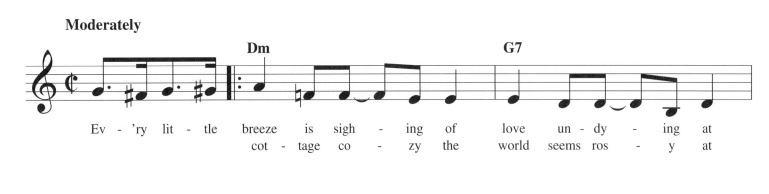

Ev - 'ry lit - tle breeze is sigh - ing of love un - dy - ing at
cot - tage co - zy the world seems ros - y at

sun - down. _____ Ev - 'ry lit - tle bird is rest - ing and
sun - down. _____ Where a lov - ing smile will greet __ me and

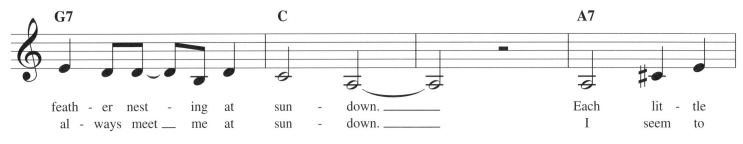

feath - er nest - ing at sun - down. _____ Each lit - tle
al - ways meet __ me at sun - down. _____ I seem to

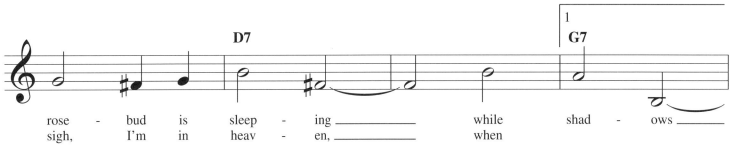

rose - bud is sleep - ing _____ while shad - ows _____
sigh, I'm in heav - en, _____ when

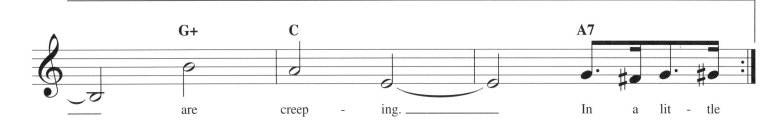

_____ are creep - ing. _____ In a lit - tle

night is fall - ing and love is call - ing me home. _____

BABY FACE

Words and Music by BENNY DAVIS
and HARRY AKST

Brightly

Ba - by face, ____ you've got the cut-est lit-tle ba - by face. _

____ There's not an - oth - er one could take your place, ____

ba - by face. ____ My poor heart ____ is jump - in',

you sure have start - ed some - thin', ba - by face. ____

I'm up in heav - en when I'm in your fond em - brace. ____

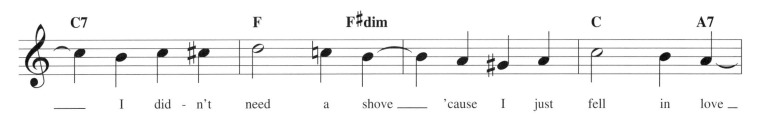

____ I did - n't need a shove ____ 'cause I just fell in love ____

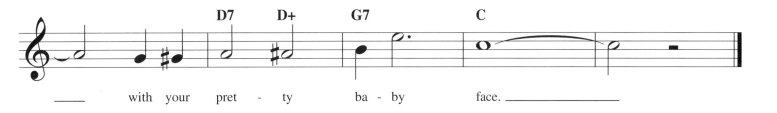

____ with your pret - ty ba - by face. ____

BACK IN YOUR OWN BACKYARD

Words and Music by AL JOLSON,
BILLY ROSE and DAVE DREYER

THE BEST THINGS IN LIFE ARE FREE
from GOOD NEWS!

Music and Lyrics by B.G. DeSYLVA,
LEW BROWN and RAY HENDERSON

BILL
from SHOW BOAT

Words by P.G. WODEHOUSE and OSCAR HAMMERSTEIN II
Music by JEROME KERN

Moderately

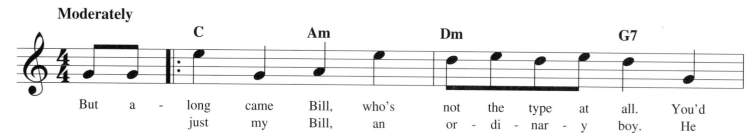

But a - long came Bill, who's not the type at all. You'd
just my Bill, an or - di - nar - y boy. He

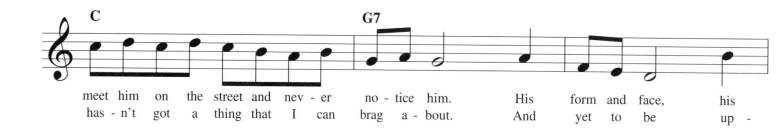

meet him on the street and nev - er no - tice him. His form and face, his
has - n't got a thing that I can brag a - bout. And yet to be up -

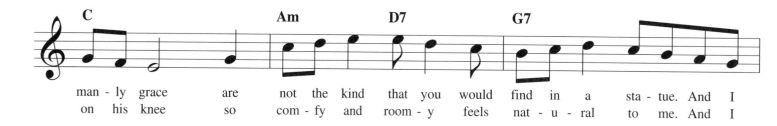

man - ly grace are not the kind that you would find in a sta - tue. And I
on his knee so com - fy and room - y feels nat - u - ral to me. And I

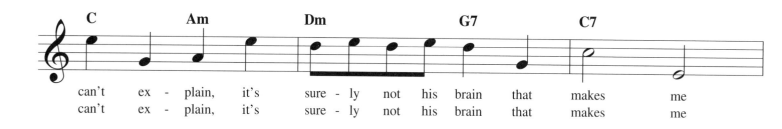

can't ex - plain, it's sure - ly not his brain that makes me
can't ex - plain, it's sure - ly not his brain that makes me

thrill.   I love him _____ be - cause he's won - der - ful, _____ be - cause he's
thrill.   I love him _____ be - cause he's I don't know, _____ be - cause he's

just old Bill.   He's
just my

Bill. _____

THE BIRTH OF THE BLUES
from GEORGE WHITE'S SCANDALS OF 1926

Words by B.G. DeSYLVA and LEW BROWN
Music by RAY HENDERSON

THE BLUE ROOM
from THE GIRL FRIEND

Words by LORENZ HART
Music by RICHARD RODGERS

BLUE SKIES

Words and Music by
IRVING BERLIN

Moderately

Blue   skies _____   smil - ing   at   me. _____
Blue - birds _____   sing - ing   a   song; _____

____ Noth - ing   but   blue   skies _____   do I   see. __
____ noth - ing   but   blue - birds _____   all day   long. _

C   E7   C   C

Nev - er   saw   the   sun   shin - ing   so   bright.

Nev - er   saw   things   go - ing   so   right.   No - tic - ing   the   days

hur - ry - ing   by;   when you're   in   love,   my   how   they   fly.

Blue   days, _____   all   of   them   gone. _____   Noth - ing   but

blue   skies _____   from   now   on. _____

BUTTON UP YOUR OVERCOAT

Words and Music by B.G. DeSYLVA,
LEW BROWN and RAY HENDERSON

Moderately

But - ton   up   your   o - ver - coat ____
But - ton   up   your   o - ver - coat ____

when   the   wind   is   free.   Take   good ____
when   the   wind   is   free.   Take   good ____

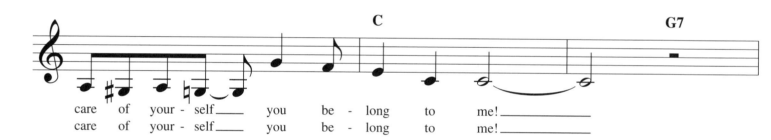

care   of   your - self ____ you   be - long   to   me! ____
care   of   your - self ____ you   be - long   to   me! ____

Eat   an   ap - ple   ev - 'ry   day; ____   get   to   bed   by
Wear   your   flan - nel   un - der - wear ____   when   you   climb   a

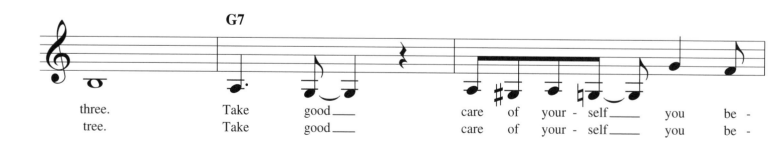

three.   Take   good ____   care   of   your - self ____ you   be -
tree.   Take   good ____   care   of   your - self ____ you   be -

long   to   me! ____   Be   care - ful   cross - ing   streets
long   to   me! ____   Don't   sit   on   hor - nets'   trails

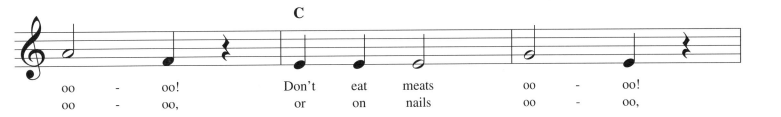

oo - oo! Don't eat meats oo - oo!
oo - oo, or on nails oo - oo,

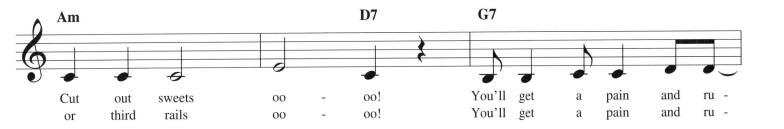

Cut out sweets oo - oo! You'll get a pain and ru -
or third rails oo - oo! You'll get a pain and ru -

- in your tum - tum! Keep a - way from
- in your tum - tum! Don't go out with

boot - leg hootch____ when you're on a spree.
col - lege boys____ when you're on a spree.

Take good____ care of your - self____ you be -
Take good____ care of your - self____ you be -

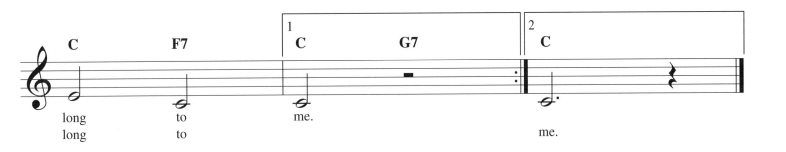

long to me.
long to me.

BYE BYE BLACKBIRD
from PETE KELLY'S BLUES

Lyric by MORT DIXON
Music by RAY HENDERSON

CALIFORNIA, HERE I COME

Words and Music by AL JOLSON
B.G. DeSYLVA and JOSEPH MEYER

CAN'T HELP LOVIN' DAT MAN

from SHOW BOAT

Lyrics by OSCAR HAMMERSTEIN II
Music by JEROME KERN

Slowly

Fish got - ta swim and birds got - ta fly. I got - ta love one man till I die.
Tell me he's la - zy, tell me he's slow. Tell me I'm cra - zy, may - be I know.

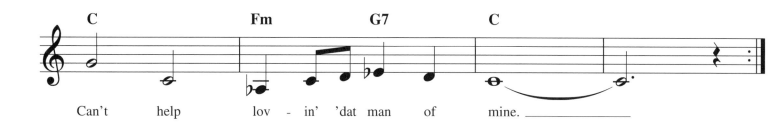

Can't help lov - in' 'dat man of mine. _____

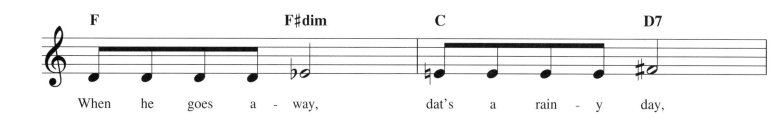

When he goes a - way, dat's a rain - y day,

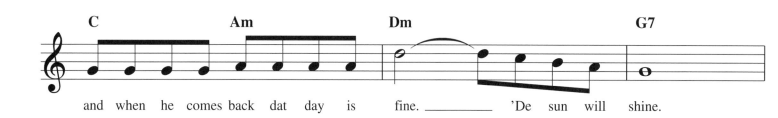

and when he comes back dat day is fine. _____ 'De sun will shine.

He can come home as late as can be. Home with-out him ain't no home to me.

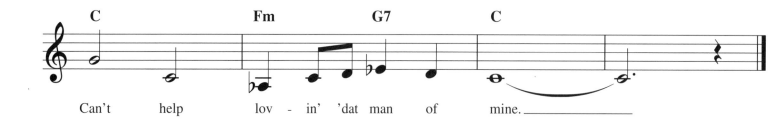

Can't help lov - in' 'dat man of mine. _____

CAROLINA MOON

Lyric by BENNY DAVIS
Music by JOE BURKE

Moderately slow

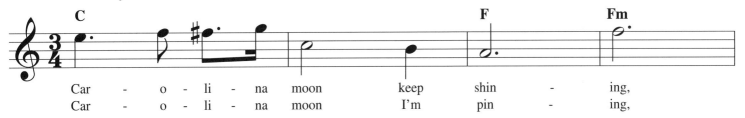

Car - o - li - na moon keep shin - ing,
Car - o - li - na moon I'm pin - ing,

shin - ing on the one who waits for me. _____
pin - ing for the place I long to be. _____

_____ How I'm hop - ing to-night you'll go, go to the right

win - dow, scat - ter your light, say I'm all right, please do. _____

_____ Tell her that I'm blue and lone -

ly, dream - y Car - o - li - na moon. _____

CHARMAINE

Words and Music by LEW POLLACK
and ERNO RAPEE

COLLEGIATE

Words and Music by MOE JAFFE
and NAT BONX

'DEED I DO

Words and Music by WALTER HIRSCH
and FRED ROSE

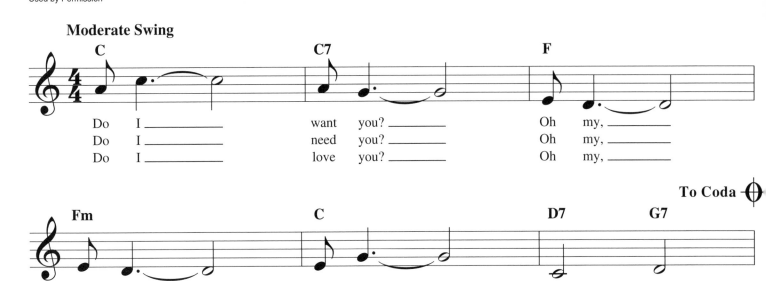

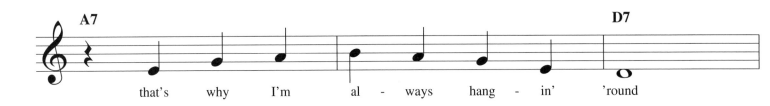

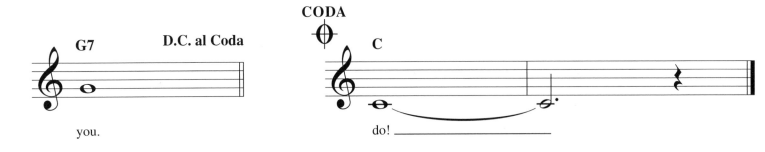

EVERYBODY LOVES MY BABY
(But My Baby Don't Love Nobody But Me)

Words and Music by JACK PALMER
and SPENCER WILLIAMS

FIVE FOOT TWO, EYES OF BLUE
(Has Anybody Seen My Girl?)

Words by JOE YOUNG and SAM LEWIS
Music by RAY HENDERSON

GEE BABY, AIN'T I GOOD TO YOU

Lyrics by DON REDMAN and ANDY RAZAF
Music by DON REDMAN

Slow Blues

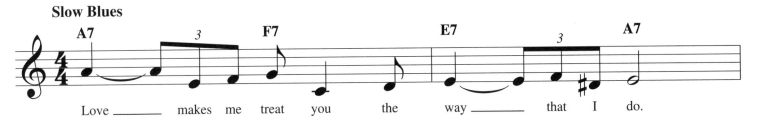

Love _____ makes me treat you the way _____ that I do.

Gee ba - by, ain't I good _ to you! There's noth - in' too good for a

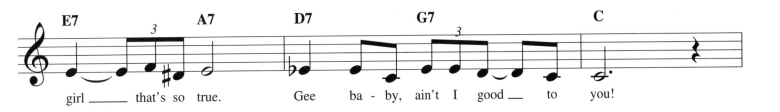

girl _____ that's so true. Gee ba - by, ain't I good _ to you!

Brought you a fur - coat for Christ - mas, a dia - mond ring, _

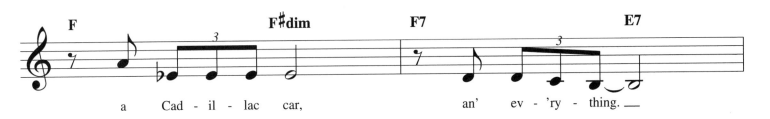

a Cad - il - lac car, an' ev - 'ry - thing. _

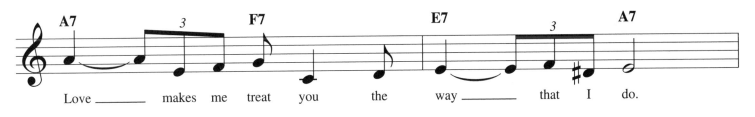

Love _____ makes me treat you the way _____ that I do.

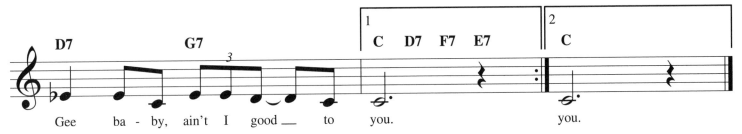

Gee ba - by, ain't I good _ to you. you.

HALLELUJAH
from HIT THE DECK

Words and Music by CLIFFORD GREY, LEO ROBIN,
and VINCENT YOUMANS

HERE COMES THE SHOW BOAT

Words by BILLY ROSE
Music by MACEO PINKARD

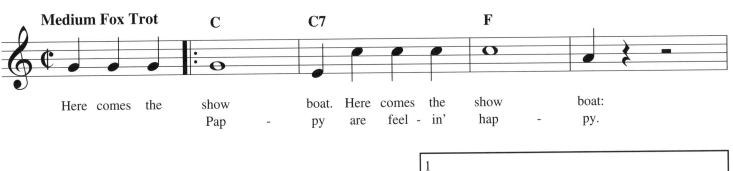

Here comes the show boat. Here comes the show boat:
Pap - py are feel - in' hap - py.

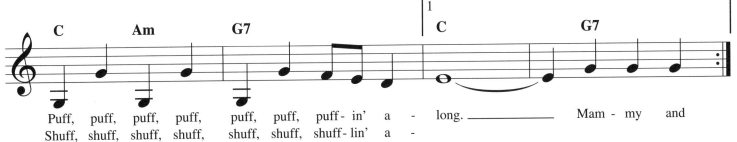

Puff, puff, puff, puff, puff, puff, puff-in' a - long. _____ Mam - my and
Shuff, shuff, shuff, shuff, shuff, shuff, shuff-lin' a -

long, _____ each lit - tle choc - 'late bon, bon, bon, bon bud - dy's in right. _____

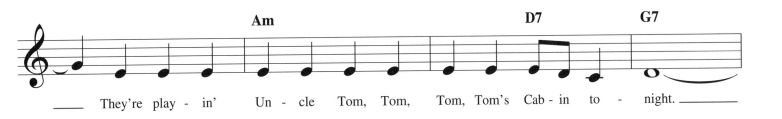

_____ They're play - in' Un - cle Tom, Tom, Tom, Tom's Cab - in to - night. _____

_____ Here comes the show boat. Here comes the show boat.

Puff, puff, puff, puff, puff, puff, puff - in' a - long. _____

THE HAWAIIAN WEDDING SONG
(Ke Kali Nei Au)

English Lyrics by AL HOFFMAN and DICK MANNING
Hawaiian Lyrics and Music by CHARLES E. KING

Slowly, warmly

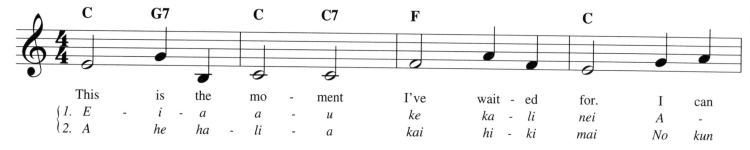

This is the mo - ment I've wait - ed for. I can
1. E - i - a a - u ke ka - li nei A -
2. A he ha - li - a kai hi - ki mai No kun

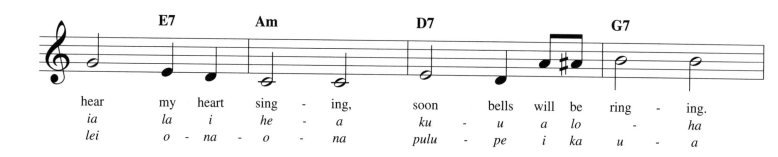

hear my heart sing - ing, soon bells will be ring - ing.
ia la i he - a ku - u a lo - ha
lei o - na - o - na pulu - pe i ka u - a

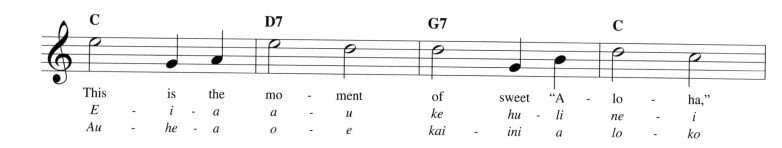

This is the mo - ment of sweet "A - lo - ha,"
E - i - a a - u ke hu - li ne - i
Au - he a o - e kai - ini a lo - ko

I will love you long - er than for - ev - er,   prom - ise me that you will leave me
A lo - a - a o - e e ka i - po   Ma - ha ka i - i - ni a ka
Nu lo - ko a - e ka ma - na - o   Hu - 'e lu - ni a - na i kuu

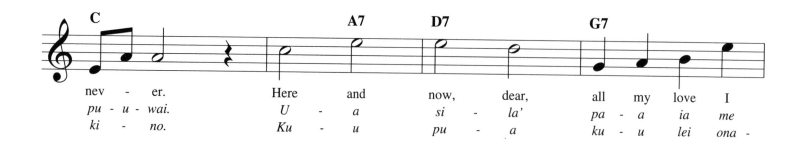

nev - er.   Here and now, dear, all my love I
pu - u - wai.   U - a si - la' pa - a ia me
ki - no.   Ku - u pu - a ku - u lei ona -

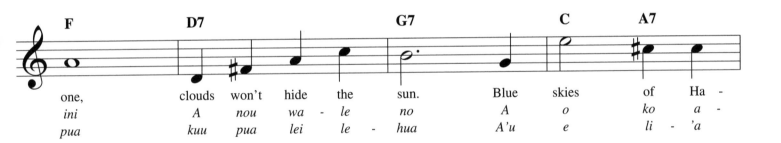

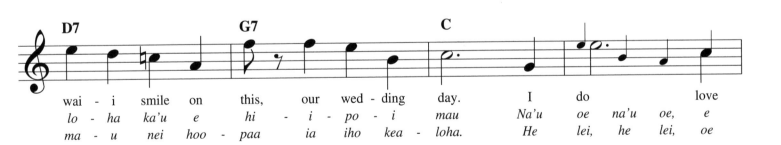

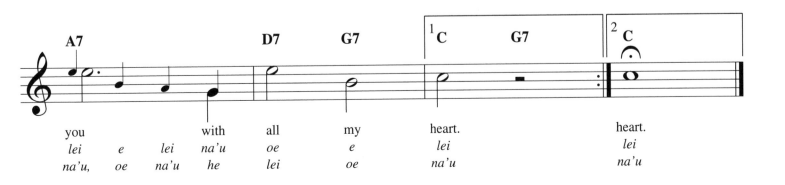

HONEY

Words and Music by RICHARD A. WHITING,
SEYMOUR SIMONS and HAVEN GILLESPIE

Moderately

I'm in love with you, Hon - ey. Say you love me too,

Hon - ey. No one else will do, Hon - ey, seems

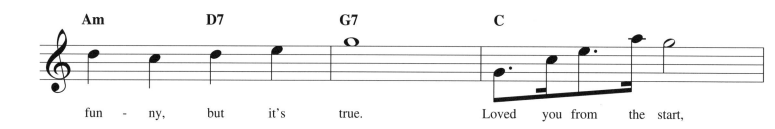

fun - ny, but it's true. Loved you from the start,

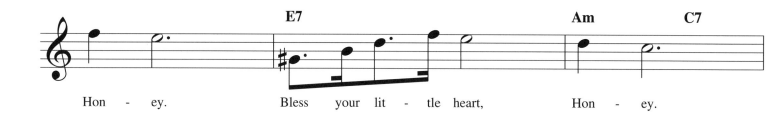

Hon - ey. Bless your lit - tle heart, Hon - ey.

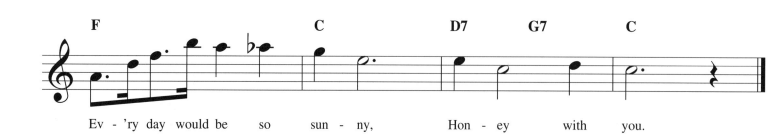

Ev - 'ry day would be so sun - ny, Hon - ey with you.

HONEYSUCKLE ROSE

Words by ANDY RAZAF
Music by THOMAS "FATS" WALLER

I CAN'T BELIEVE THAT YOU'RE IN LOVE WITH ME

Words and Music by JIMMY McHUGH
and CLARENCE GASKILL

Your eyes of blue, your kiss - es too, I nev - er knew what
tell - ing ev - 'ry - one I know, I'm on your mind each

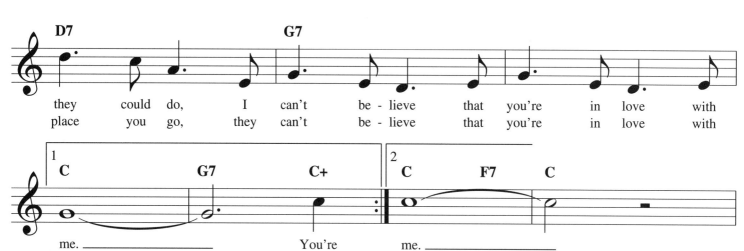

they could do, I can't be - lieve that you're in love with
place you go, they can't be - lieve that you're in love with

me. _____ You're
me. _____

I have al - ways placed you far a - bove me.

I just can't i - mag - ine that you love me. And

af - ter all is said and done, to think that I'm the luck - y one, I

can't be - lieve that you're in love with me. _____

I CAN'T GIVE YOU ANYTHING BUT LOVE
from BLACKBIRDS OF 1928

Words and Music by JIMMY McHUGH
and DOROTHY FIELDS

I CRIED FOR YOU

Words and Music by ARTHUR FREED,
GUS ARNHEIM and ABE LYMAN

I LOVE MY BABY
(My Baby Loves Me)

Words by BUD GREEN
Music by HARRY WARREN

I WANNA BE LOVED BY YOU

Lyrics by BERT KALMAR
Music by HERBERT STOTHART and HARRY RUBY

Moderately

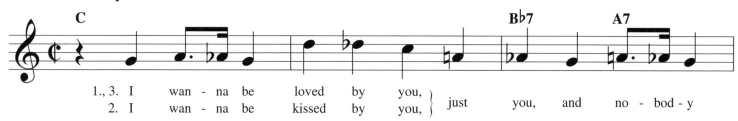

1., 3. I wan - na be loved by you,
2. I wan - na be kissed by you, } just you, and no - bod - y

else but you.
{ I wan - na be loved by you a -
{ I wan - na be kissed by you a

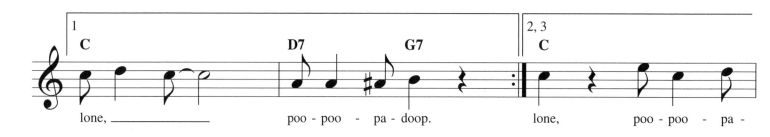

lone, _____ poo - poo - pa - doop. lone, poo - poo - pa -

Fine

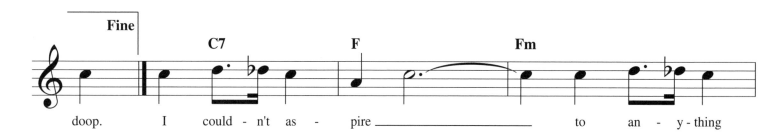

doop. I could - n't as - pire _____ to an - y - thing

high - er, _____ than fill a de - sire _____ to

D.C. al Fine

make you my own; pa - pa - pad - ra, poo - poo - pa - doop.

I'LL GET BY
(As Long As I Have You)

Lyrics by ROY TURK
Music by FRED E. AHLERT

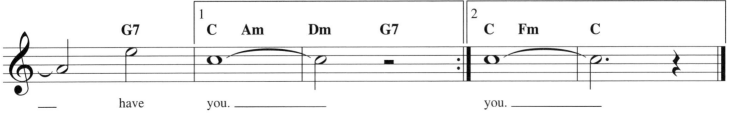

I'M LOOKING OVER A FOUR LEAF CLOVER

Lyric by MORT DIXON
Music by HARRY WOODS

Brightly

I'm look - ing o - ver a four leaf clo -

- ver that I o - ver - looked be - fore. _____

One leaf is sun - shine, the sec - ond is rain, _____

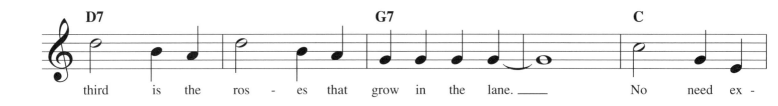

third is the ros - es that grow in the lane. _____ No need ex -

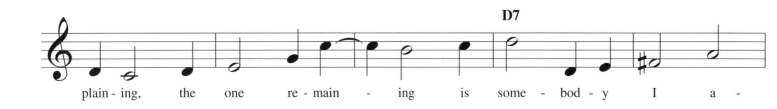

plain - ing, the one re - main - ing is some - bod - y I a -

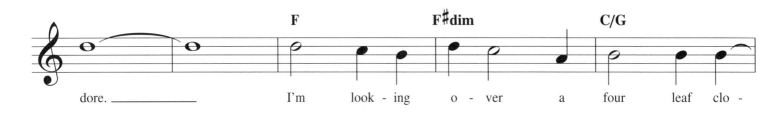

dore. _____ I'm look - ing o - ver a four leaf clo -

- ver that I o - ver - looked be - fore. _____

I'M SITTING ON TOP OF THE WORLD
from THE JOLSON STORY

Words by SAM M. LEWIS and JOE YOUNG
Music by RAY HENDERSON

I'VE FOUND A NEW BABY
(I Found a New Baby)

Words and Music by JACK PALMER
and SPENCER WILLIAMS

Brightly, not too fast

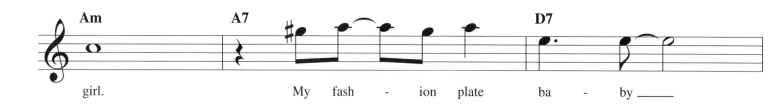

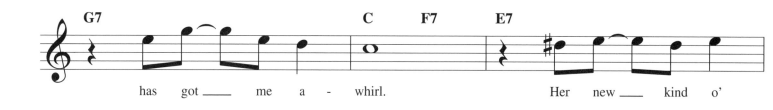

C crave. **E7** Sweet - est miss, with a

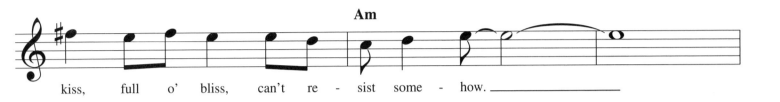

kiss, full o' bliss, can't re - sist some - how. **Am**

D7 Tells me lies, but she's wise, naught - y eyes mes - mer -

G ize I vow. And **E7** how! I don't mean may - **Am** be,

E7 I just had to fall. **Am** **A7** I've found a new

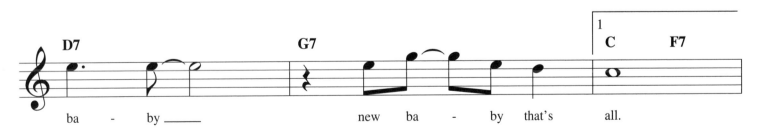

D7 ba - by **G7** new ba - by that's all. **1** **C** **F7**

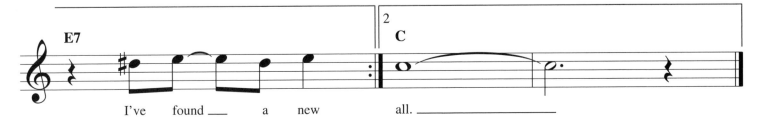

E7 I've found a new **2** **C** all.

IF YOU KNEW SUSIE
(Like I Know Susie)

Words and Music by B.G. DeSYLVA
and JOSEPH MEYER

IN A LITTLE SPANISH TOWN
('Twas on a Night Like This)

Words by SAM M. LEWIS and JOE YOUNG
Music by MABEL WAYNE

IF YOU WERE THE ONLY GIRL IN THE WORLD

Words by CLIFFORD GREY
Music by NAT D. AYER

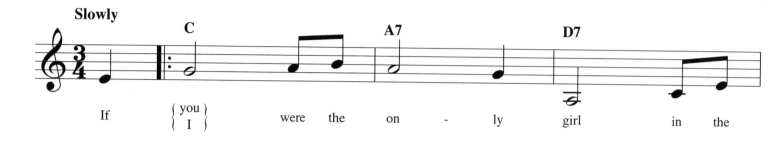

Slowly

C   A7   D7

If   { you / I }   were the on - ly girl in the

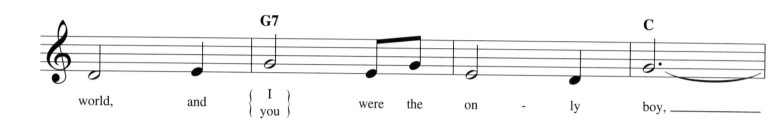

G7   C

world,   and   { I / you }   were the on - ly boy, _____

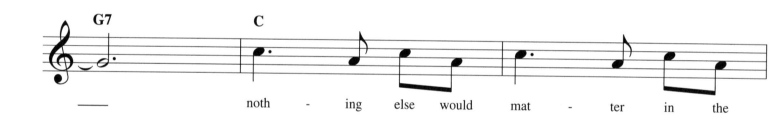

G7   C

____ noth - ing else would mat - ter in the

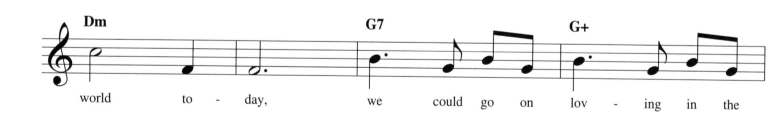

Dm   G7   G+

world to - day,   we could go on lov - ing in the

C   A7

same old way.   A Gar - den of E - den

INDIAN LOVE CALL

Lyrics by OTTO HARBACH and OSCAR HAMMERSTEIN II
Music by RUDOLF FRIML

IT ALL DEPENDS ON YOU
from THE SINGING FOOL

Words and Music by B.G. DeSYLVA,
LEW BROWN and RAY HENDERSON

LAST NIGHT ON THE BACK PORCH
(I Loved Her Best of All)

Words and Music by LEW BROWN
and CARL SCHRAUBSTADER

Moderately

I love her in the morn - ing and I love her at

night. {I love her, yes I love her when the
The first time that I met her it was

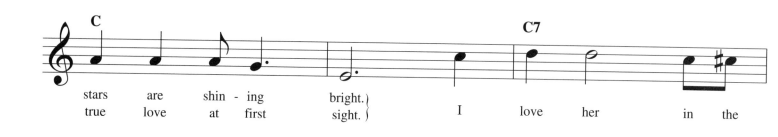

stars are shin - ing bright.) I love her in the
true love at first sight. }

spring - time and I love her in the fall, but last night {on the
in the

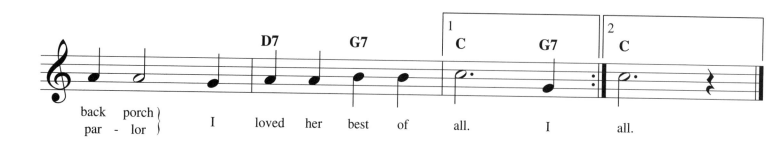

back porch} I loved her best of all. I all.
par - lor }

LET A SMILE BE YOUR UMBRELLA

Words by IRVING KAHAL and FRANCIS WHEELER
Music by SAMMY FAIN

LET ME SING AND I'M HAPPY

Words and Music by
IRVING BERLIN

Moderately

Let me sing ___ a fun-ny song ___ with cra-zy words ___ that

roll a - long. ___ And if my song ___ can start you laugh-ing, I'm

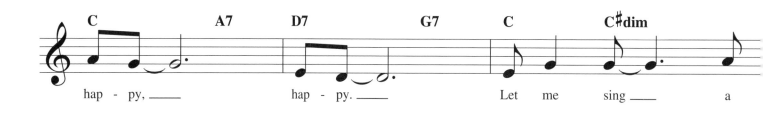

hap - py, ___ hap - py. ___ Let me sing ___ a

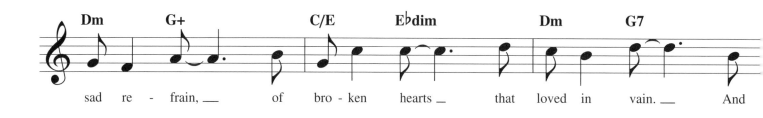

sad re - frain, ___ of bro - ken hearts ___ that loved in vain. ___ And

if my song ___ can start you cry - ing, I'm hap -

py.   Let   me   croon __ a   low down blues __ to

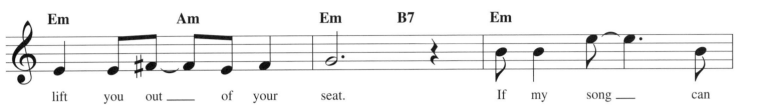

lift   you   out ___ of   your   seat.   If   my   song __ can

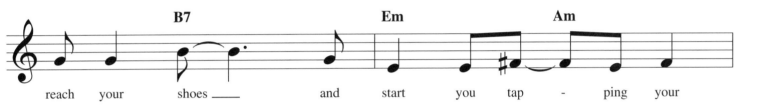

reach your   shoes ___ and   start   you   tap - ping your

feet, I'm hap - py.   Let   me   sing ___ of Dix - ie's   charms, __ the

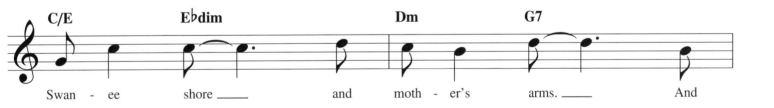

Swan - ee   shore ___ and moth - er's   arms. ___ And

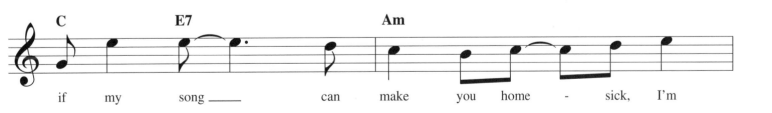

if   my   song ___ can make   you home - sick, I'm

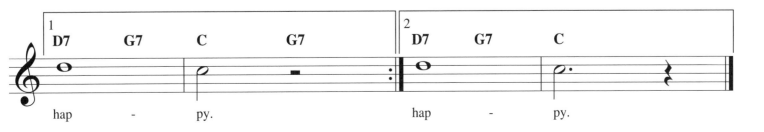

hap -   py.   hap -   py.

LINGER AWHILE

Lyric by HARRY OWENS
Music by VINCENT ROSE

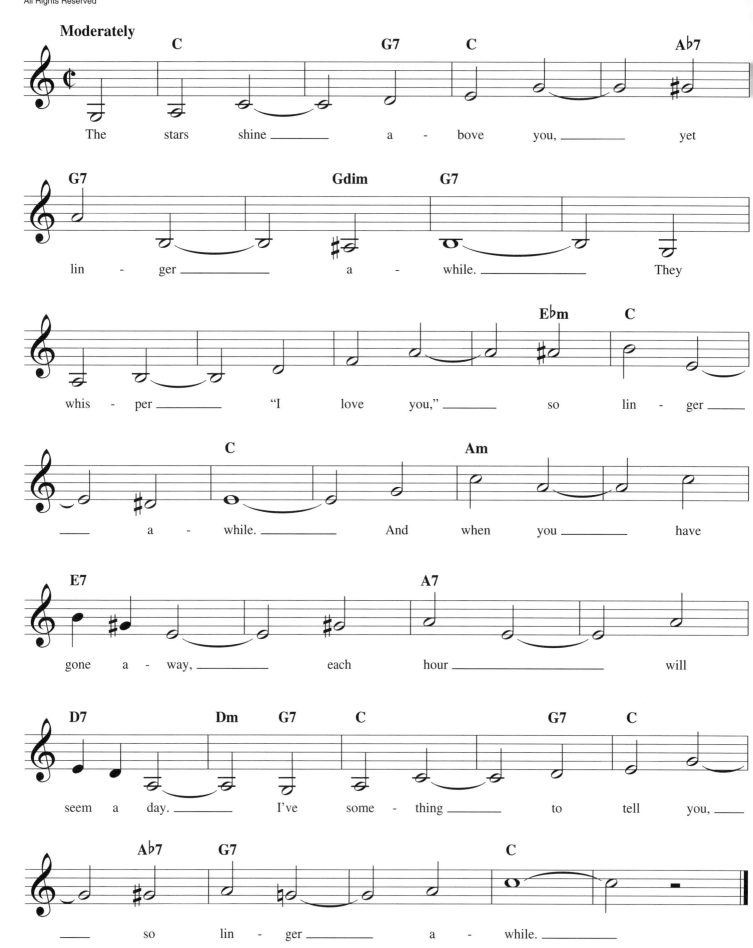

LOUISE

Words by LEO ROBIN
Music by RICHARD A. WHITING

LOVE ME OR LEAVE ME
from LOVE ME OR LEAVE ME

Lyrics by GUS KAHN
Music by WALTER DONALDSON

LOVER, COME BACK TO ME
from THE NEW MOON

Lyrics by OSCAR HAMMERSTEIN II
Music by SIGMUND ROMBERG

Moderately

The sky was blue, and high a-bove the moon was new, and so was love.
You came at last, love had its day, that day is past, you've gone a-way.

This ea-ger heart of mine was sing — ing: "Lov-er, where can you
This ach-ing heart of mine is sing — ing: "Lov-er, come back to

be?" _____ me!" When I re-mem-ber ev-'ry lit-tle thing you used to do,

I'm so lone-ly. Ev-'ry road I walk a-long I've walked a-long with you.

No won-der I am lone-ly. The sky is blue, the night is cold,

the moon is new but love is old. And while I'm wait-ing here, this

heart of mine is sing — ing: "Lov-er, come back to me!" _____

MAKE BELIEVE
from SHOW BOAT

Lyrics by OSCAR HAMMERSTEIN II
Music by JEROME KERN

We could make be - lieve _____ I love you, _____ on - ly

make be - lieve _____ that you love me. _____ Oth - ers

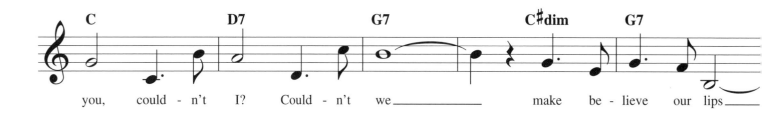

find peace of mind in pre - tend - ing. _____ Could - n't

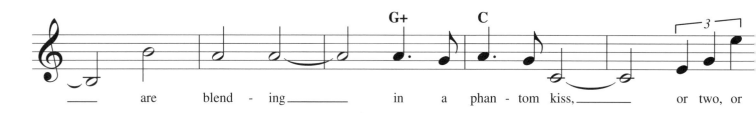

you, could - n't I? Could - n't we _____ make be - lieve our lips _____

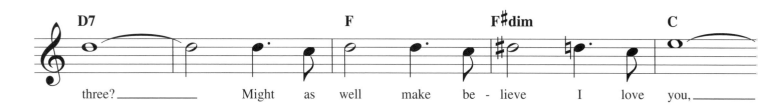

_____ are blend - ing _____ in a phan - tom kiss, _____ or two, or

three? _____ Might as well make be - lieve I love you, _____

for to tell the truth, _____ I do. _____

MAKIN' WHOOPEE!

Lyrics by GUS KAHN
Music by WALTER DONALDSON

MANHATTAN

Words by LORENZ HART
Music by RICHARD RODGERS

MARIE

Words and Music by
IRVING BERLIN

Moderately

Ma - rie, _____ the dawn is break - ing. Ma -

rie, _____ you'll soon be wak - ing to

find _____ your heart is ach - ing, And

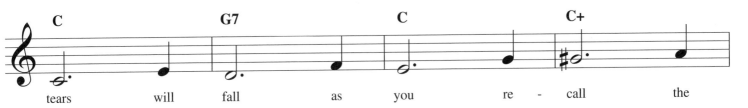

tears will fall as you re - call the

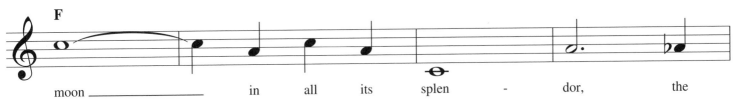

moon _____ in all its splen - dor, the

kiss _____ so ver - y ten - der, the

words _____ will you sur - ren - der, to

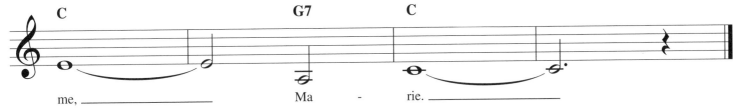

me, _____ Ma - rie. _____

MEAN TO ME

Lyric and Music by FRED E. AHLERT
and ROY TURK

MEXICALI ROSE
from MEXICALI ROSE

Words by HELEN STONE
Music by JACK B. TENNEY

Waltz tempo

Mex - i - cal - i   Rose,   stop   cry - ing;

I'll   come   back   to   you   some   sun - ny   day.

Ev - 'ry   night   you'll   know   that   I'll   be   pin - ing,

ev - 'ry   hour   a   year   while   I'm   a - way.

Dry   those   big   brown   eyes   and   smile,   dear.

Ban - ish   all   those   tears   and   please   don't   sigh.

Kiss   me   once   a - gain   and   hold   me;

Mex - i - cal - i   Rose   good - bye.

MISS YOU

Words by CHARLES TOBIAS and HARRY TOBIA
Music by HENRY H. TOBIA

MOONLIGHT AND ROSES
(Bring Mem'ries of You)

Words and Music by BEN BLACK,
EDWIN H. LEMARE and NEIL MORET

MISSISSIPPI MUD

Words and Music by JAMES CAVANAUGH
and HARRY BARRIS

Moderately slow, with a beat

When the sun goes down the tide goes out. The

peo - ple gath - er 'round and they all be - gin to shout

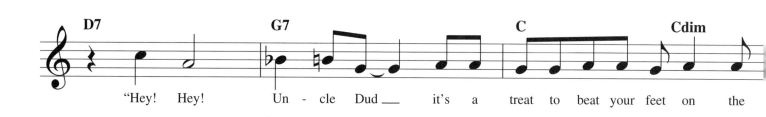

"Hey! Hey! Un - cle Dud ___ it's a treat to beat your feet on the

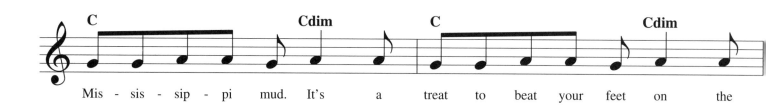

Mis - sis - sip - pi mud. It's a treat to beat your feet on the

Mis - sis - sip - pi mud." What a dance ___ do they do! ___

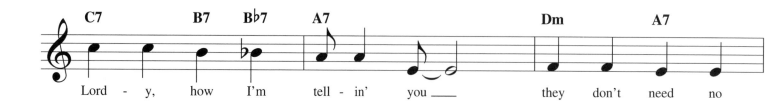

Lord - y, how I'm tell - in' you ___ they don't need no

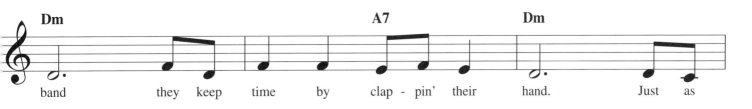

band   they   keep   time   by   clap - pin' their   hand.   Just   as

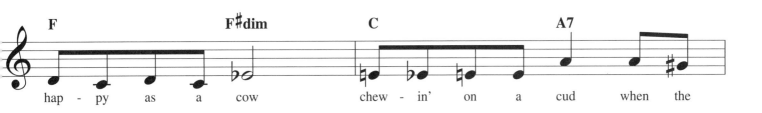

hap - py   as   a   cow   chew - in'   on   a   cud   when   the

peo - ple   beat   their   feet   on   the   Mis - sis - sip - pi   mud.

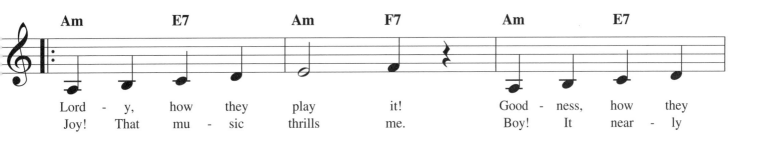

Lord - y,   how   they   play   it!   Good - ness,   how   they
Joy!   That   mu - sic   thrills   me.   Boy!   It   near - ly

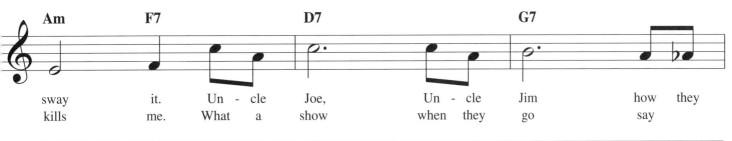

sway   it.   Un - cle   Joe,   Un - cle   Jim   how   they
kills   me.   What   a   show   when   they   go   say

pound   the   mire _____ with   vig - or   and   vim.

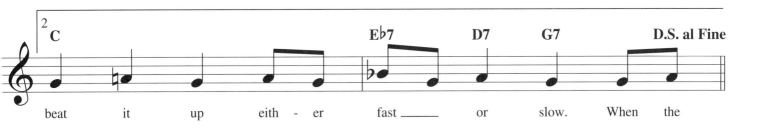

beat   it   up   eith - er   fast _____ or   slow.   When   the

MORE THAN YOU KNOW

Words by WILLIAM ROSE and EDWARD ELISC
Music by VINCENT YOUMAN

MOUNTAIN GREENERY
from the Broadway Musical THE GARRICK GAIETIES

Words by LORENZ HART
Music by RICHARD RODGERS

MY BLUE HEAVEN

Lyric by GEORGE WHITING
Music by WALTER DONALDSON

MY HEART STOOD STILL
from A CONNECTICUT YANKEE

Words by LORENZ HART
Music by RICHARD RODGERS

MY LUCKY STAR

Words and Music by B.G. DeSYLVA,
LEW BROWN and RAY HENDERSON

Moderately

I'd like to find my luck-y star, _____ its ti-ny light has

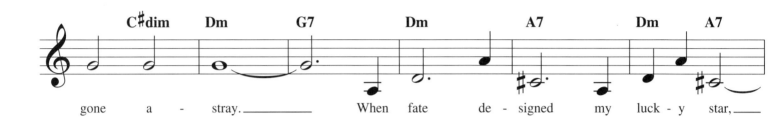

gone a - stray. _____ When fate de - signed my luck-y star, _____

_____ there must have been a hol - i - day. _____ Why can't I

be as oth - ers are _____ whose lives are like the month of

May? _____ Be good to me, my luck - y star, _____

_____ and send the one I love my way! _____

MY MAN

Words and Music by JAMES HANLEY
and GENE BUCK

Moderately

My man _____ no one can love me like he can, _____ and that's the rea - son why

I know _____ I love him so. _____ His love I

treas - ure _____ be - cause he gives me good meas - ure, _____ and then he gives me such

pleas - ure _____ like no one can. _____

I rave _____ so much a - bout him 'cause I crave _____ the style of lov - ing that

he's shown _____ when we're a - lone. _____ I'll leave him

nev - er, _____ I'm goin' to love him for - ev - er. _____ And there is noth - ing can

sev - er _____ me from my man. _____

OL' MAN RIVER
from SHOW BOAT

Lyrics by OSCAR HAMMERSTEIN II
Music by JEROME KERN

Slowly

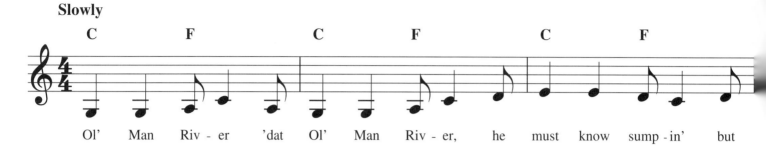

Ol' Man Riv - er 'dat Ol' Man Riv - er, he must know sump -in' but

don't say noth -in'. He jus' keeps roll - in', he keeps on roll - in' a -

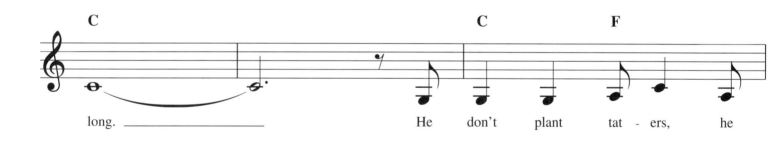

long. _____ He don't plant tat - ers, he

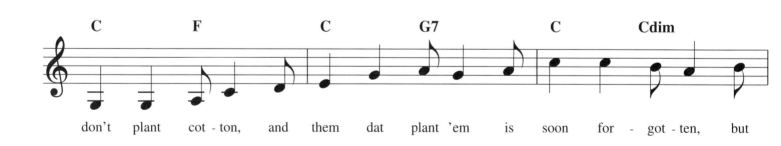

don't plant cot - ton, and them dat plant 'em is soon for - got - ten, but

Ol' Man Riv - er, he just keeps roll - in' a - long. _____

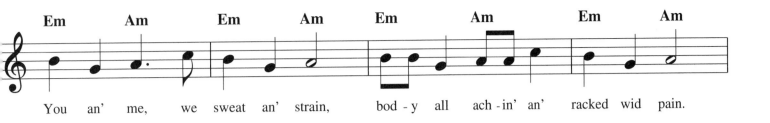

You an' me, we sweat an' strain, bod-y all ach-in' an' racked wid pain.

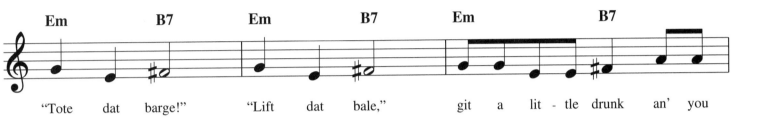

"Tote dat barge!" "Lift dat bale," git a lit-tle drunk an' you

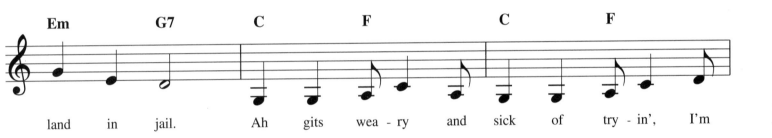

land in jail. Ah gits wea-ry and sick of try-in', I'm

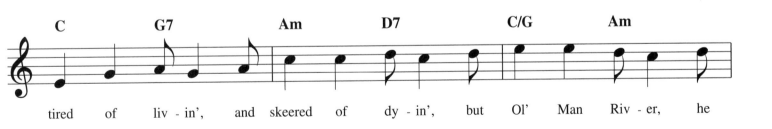

tired of liv-in', and skeered of dy-in', but Ol' Man Riv-er, he

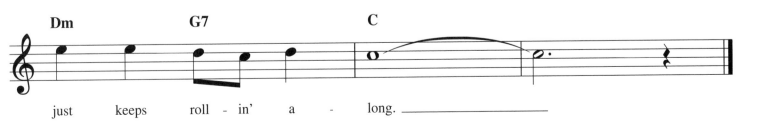

just keeps roll-in' a - long. _____

PADDLIN' MADELIN' HOME

Words and Music by
HARRY WOODS

'Cause when I'm pad - dl - in' Ma - de - lin'

home _____ Gee! when I'm pad - dl - in' Ma -

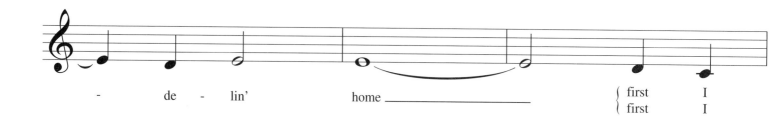

- de - lin' home _____ { first   I
                          { first   I

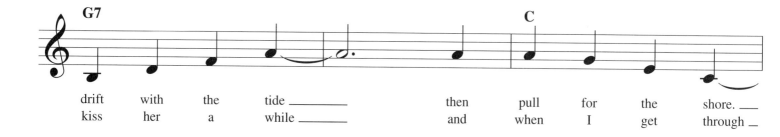

drift with the tide _____ then pull for the shore. __
kiss her a while _____ and when I get through __

__   I hug her and kiss _____ her and
__   I pad - dle for one _____ mile and

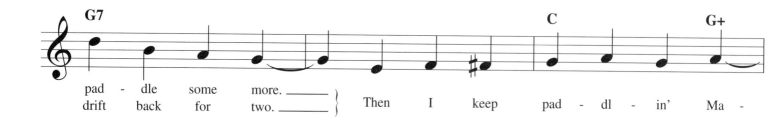

pad - dle some more. _____ } Then I keep pad - dl - in' Ma -
drift back for two. _____ }

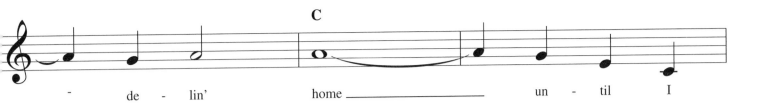

- de - lin'   home _____ un - til I

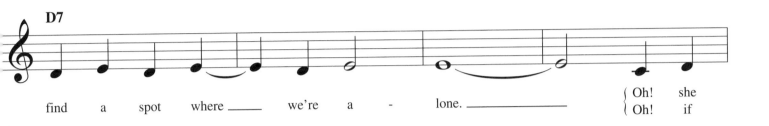

find   a   spot   where ____ we're a - lone. _____ { Oh! she
                                                                  { Oh! if

nev - er says "no" _____ so   I   kiss her and go ____
she'd on - ly say _____ throw your pad - dles a - way ____

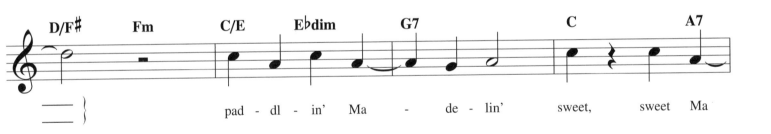

____ }   pad - dl - in' Ma - de - lin' sweet, sweet Ma

- de - lin'   pad - dl - in' Ma - de - lin'

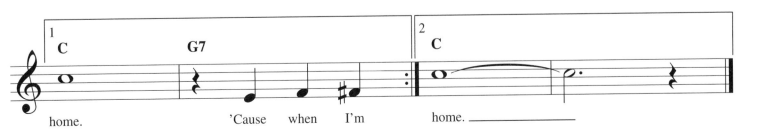

home.   'Cause when I'm   home. _____

PUTTIN' ON THE RITZ
from the Motion Picture PUTTIN' ON THE RITZ

Words and Music by
IRVING BERLIN

Moderate Swing

If you're blue and you ____ don't know where to go to, why don't you go where fash - ion

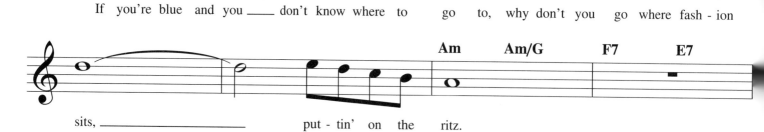

sits, _____ put - tin' on the ritz.

Dif - f'rent types who wear ____ a day coat, pants with stripes and cut - a - way coat, per - fect

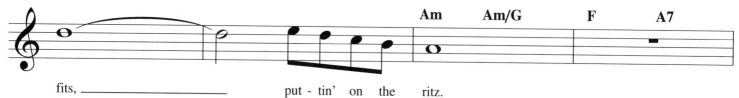

fits, _____ put - tin' on the ritz.

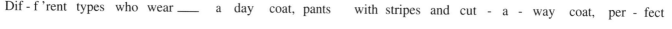

Stroll - ing up the a - ve - nue so hap - py. ____
(Alt: Dressed up like a mil - lion dol - lar troup - er. ____

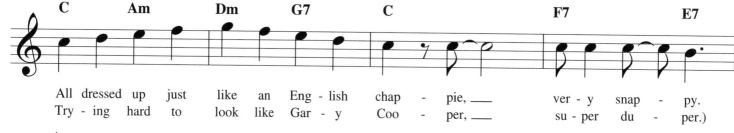

All dressed up just like an Eng - lish chap - pie, ____ ver - y snap - py.
Try - ing hard to look like Gar - y Coo - per, ____ su - per du - per.)

Come let's mix where Rock - e - fel - lers walk with sticks or "um - ber - el - las" in their

mitts, _____ put - tin' on the ritz. _____   ritz. _____

ROCKIN' CHAIR

Words and Music by
HOAGY CARMICHAEL

Moderately

SAY IT WITH MUSIC
from the 1921 Stage Production MUSIC BOX REVUE

Words and Music by
IRVING BERLIN

Moderately

Say it with mu - sic, beau - ti - ful

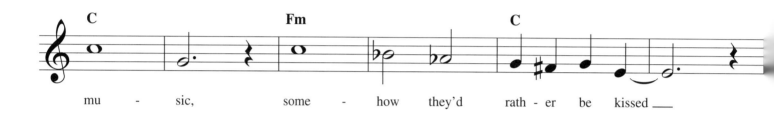

mu - sic, some - how they'd rath - er be kissed ___

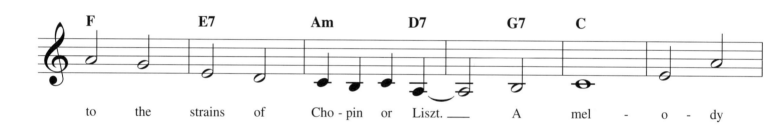

to the strains of Cho - pin or Liszt. ___ A mel - o - dy

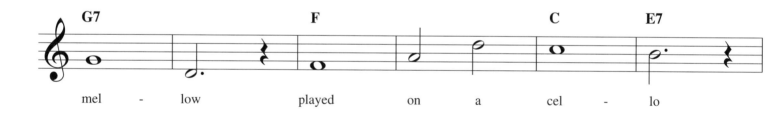

mel - low played on a cel - lo

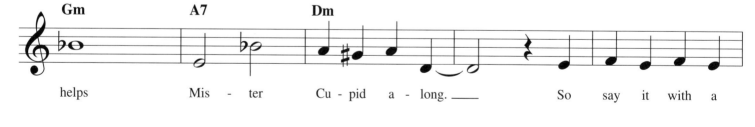

helps Mis - ter Cu - pid a - long. ___ So say it with a

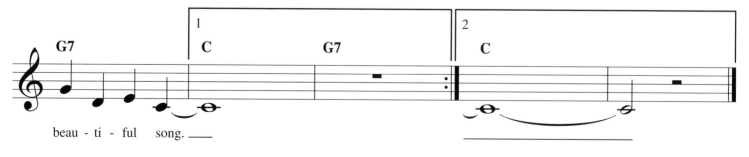

beau - ti - ful song. ___

SENTIMENTAL ME
from the Broadway Musical THE GARRICK GAIETIES

Words by LORENZ HART
Music by RICHARD RODGERS

Oh, sen - ti - men - tal me and poor ro - man - tic you; _____

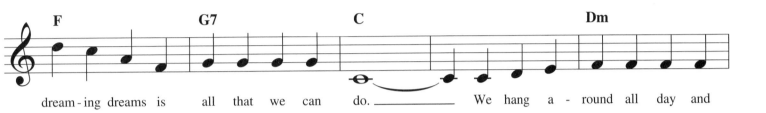

dream - ing dreams is all that we can do. _____ We hang a - round all day and

pon - der, while both of us grow fond - er. The Lord knows where we're wan - der - ing

to! _____ I sit and sigh; you sigh and sit up - on ___ my knee. ___

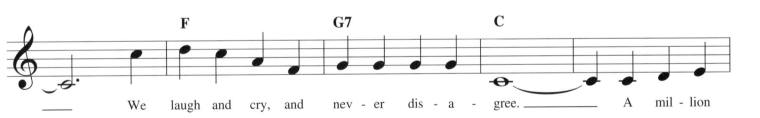

_____ We laugh and cry, and nev - er dis - a - gree. _____ A mil - lion

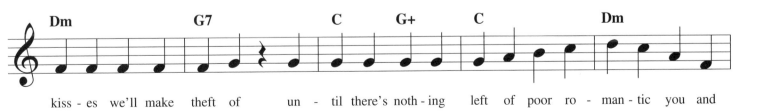

kiss - es we'll make theft of un - til there's noth - ing left of poor ro - man - tic you and

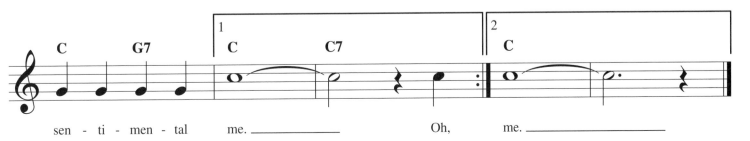

sen - ti - men - tal me. _____ Oh, me. _____

SIDE BY SIDE

Words and Music by
HARRY WOODS

Moderately

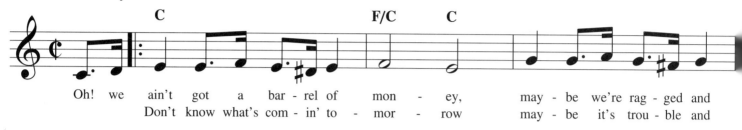

Oh! we ain't got a bar-rel of mon - ey, may - be we're rag - ged and
Don't know what's com - in' to - mor - row may - be it's trou - ble and

fun - ny. But we'll trav - el a - long ___ sing - in' a song ___
sor - row. But we'll trav - el the road ___ shar - in' our load ___

side by side. Through all kinds of weath - er what if the sky should

fall. Just as long as we're to geth - er, it does - n't mat - ter at

all. When they've all had their quar - rels and part - ed

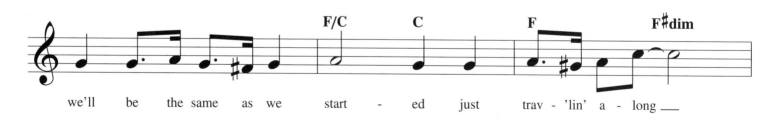

we'll be the same as we start - ed just trav - 'lin' a - long ___

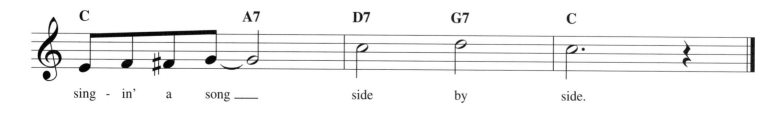

sing - in' a song ___ side by side.

SOMEBODY LOVES ME
from GEORGE WHITE'S SCANDALS OF 1924

Words by B.G. DeSYLVA and BALLARD MacDONALD
Music by GEORGE GERSHWIN

SOMETIMES I'M HAPPY

Words by CLIFFORD GREY and IRVING CAESAR
Music by VINCENT YOUMANS

Slowly

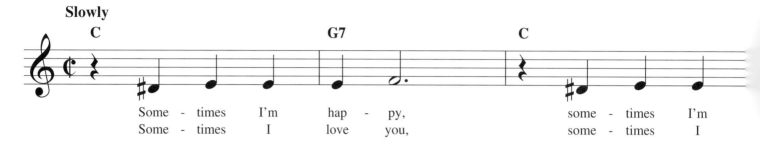

Some - times I'm hap - py, some - times I'm
Some - times I love you, some - times I

blue, _____ my dis - po - si - tion
hate you, but when I hate you

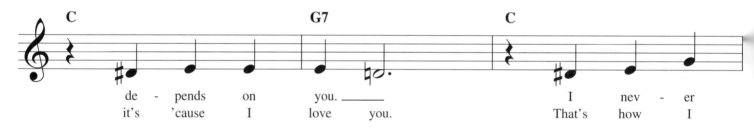

de - pends on you. _____ I nev - er
it's 'cause I love you. That's how I

mind the rain from the skies, _____ if I can
am so what can I do? _____

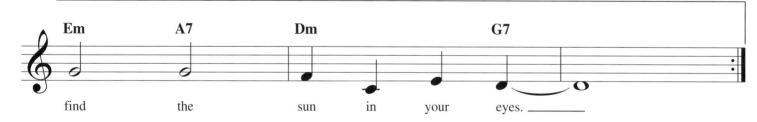

find the sun in your eyes. _____

I'm hap - py when I'm with you. _____

THE SONG IS ENDED
(But the Melody Lingers On)

Words and Music by
IRVING BERLIN

Moderate Waltz

The song _____ is end - ed, but the mel - o - dy lin - gers on.
night _____ was splen - did and the mel - o - dy seemed to say,

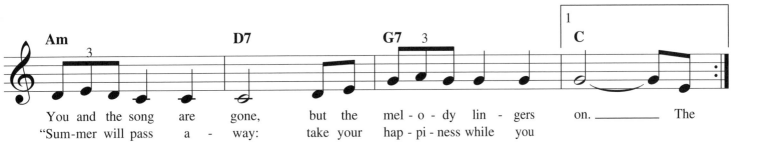

You and the song are gone, but the mel - o - dy lin - gers on. _____ The
"Sum - mer will pass a - way: take your hap - pi - ness while you

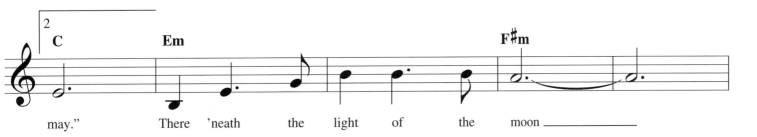

may." There 'neath the light of the moon _____

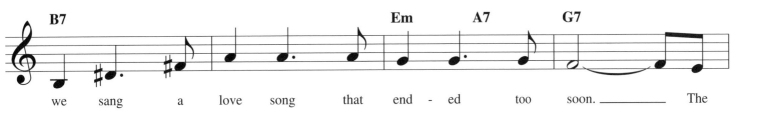

we sang a love song that end - ed too soon. _____ The

moon _____ de - scend - ed, and I found with the break of dawn,

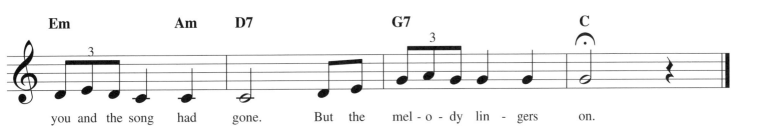

you and the song had gone. But the mel - o - dy lin - gers on.

STARDUST

Words by MITCHELL PARISH
Music by HOAGY CARMICHAEL

Moderately

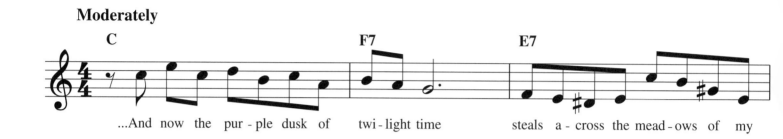

...And now the pur-ple dusk of twi-light time   steals a-cross the mead-ows of my

heart.   High up in the sky the lit-tle stars climb,

al-ways re-mind-ing me that we're a-part.   You wan-dered down the lane and

far a-way,   leav-ing me a song that will not die.

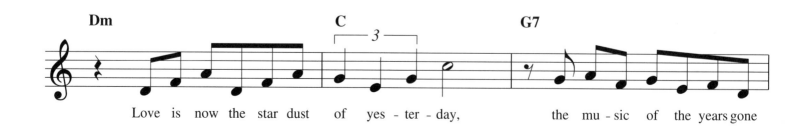

Love is now the star dust of yes-ter-day,   the mu-sic of the years gone

by. _____ Some-times I won-der why I spend the lone-ly night
side a gar-den wall when stars are bright,

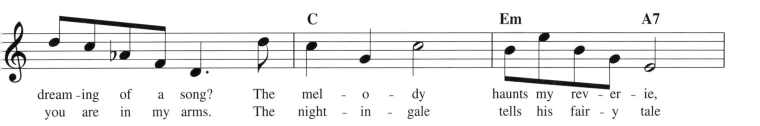

dream-ing of a song? The mel - o - dy haunts my rev-er-ie,
you are in my arms. The night - in - gale tells his fair-y tale

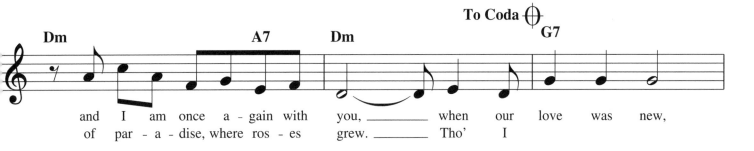

To Coda ⊕

and I am once a-gain with you, _____ when our love was new,
of par - a - dise, where ros - es grew. _____ Tho' I

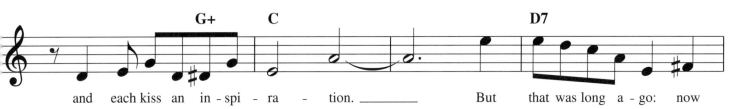

and each kiss an in-spi - ra - tion. _____ But that was long a-go: now

D.S. al Coda

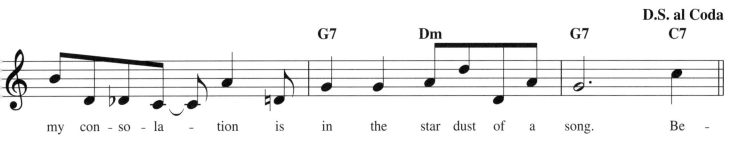

my con - so - la - tion is in the star dust of a song. Be -

CODA ⊕

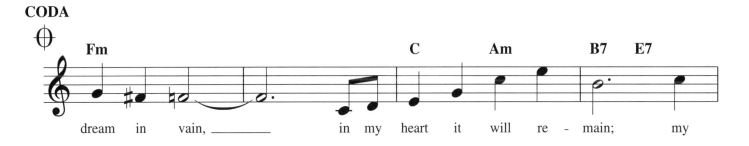

dream in vain, _____ in my heart it will re - main; my

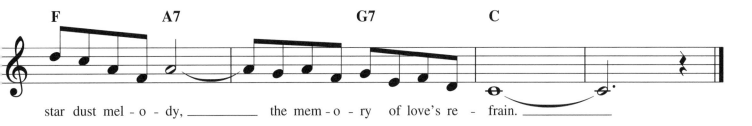

star dust mel - o - dy, _____ the mem - o - ry of love's re - frain. _____

STOUTHEARTED MEN
from THE NEW MOON

Lyrics by OSCAR HAMMERSTEIN II
Music by SIGMUND ROMBERG

March tempo

Give me some men who are stout-heart-ed men who will fight for the right they a-

dore. Start me with ten, who are stout-heart-ed men and I'll

soon give you ten thou-sand more. Oh! Shoul-der to shoul-der and

bold-der and bold-er they grow as they go to the fore!

Then _____ there's noth-ing in the world can

halt or mar a plan, _____

when _____ stout-heart-ed men _____ can stick to-

geth-er man to man! _____

SUGAR BLUES

Words by LUCY FLETCHER
Music by CLARENCE WILLIAMS

Moderate Blues tempo

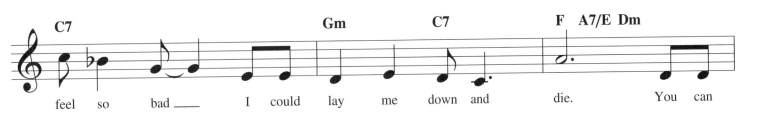

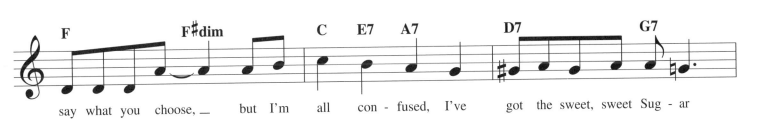

SWEET SUE – JUST YOU
from RHYTHM PARADE

Words by WILL J. HARRIS
Music by VICTOR YOUNG

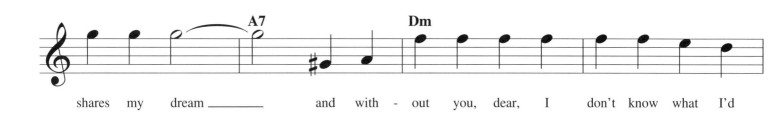

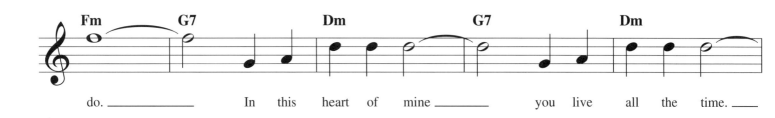

THAT'S MY WEAKNESS NOW

Words and Music by BUD GREEN
and SAM STEPT

THERE'LL BE SOME CHANGES MADE
from ALL THAT JAZZ

Words by BILLY HIGGINS
Music by W. BENTON OVERSTREET

Easy Swing

For there's a change in the weath - er there's a change in the sea, ___
change in the fash - ions, ask the fem - i - nine folks, ___

so from now on there'll be a change in me. _____ My
e - ven Jack Ben - ny has been chang - ing jokes. ___ I

walk will be dif - f'rent, my talk and my name, ___ noth - in' a - bout me is goin' to
must make some chang - es from old to the new, ___ I must do things just the same as

be the same. ___ I'm goin' to change my way of liv - in' if that ain't e - nough, ___
oth - ers do. ___ I'm goin' to change my long, tall { Mam - ma } { Dad - dy } for a little short fat, ___

then I'll change the way that I strut my stuff. ___ 'Cause no - bod - y wants ___ you when you're
goin' to change the num - ber where I live at. ___ I must have some lov - in' or I'll

old and gray, ___ there'll be some chang - es made to - day, ___
fade a - way, ___ there'll be some chang - es made to - day, ___

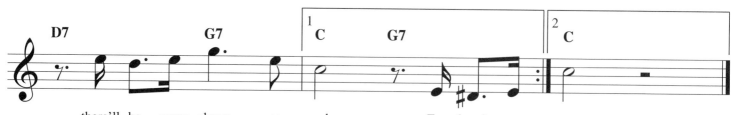

there'll be some chang - es made. For there's a
there'll be some chang - es made.

THOU SWELL
from A CONNECTICUT YANKEE

Words by LORENZ HART
Music by RICHARD RODGERS

THE VARSITY DRAG
from GOOD NEWS

Words and Music by B.G. DeSYLVA
LEW BROWN and RAY HENDERSON

WEDDING BELLS
(Are Breaking Up That Old Gang of Mine)

Words by IRVING KAHAL, and WILLIE RASKIN
Music by SAMMY FAIN

Not a soul down on the cor - ner, that's a pret - ty cer - tain
boys are sing - ing love songs, they for - got "Sweet A - de -

sign, that wed - ding bells ___ are break - ing up ___ that
line" those wed - ding bells ___ are break - ing up ___ that

old gang of mine. All the old gang of mine.

There goes Jack, ___ there goes Jim, ___ down to lov - er's lane. ___

Now and then ___ we meet a - gain, ___ but they don't seem the same. Gee I

get a lone - some feel - ing, when I hear the church bells chime, those

wed - ding bells ___ are break - ing up ___ that old gang of mine.

WHAT'LL I DO?
from MUSIC BOX REVUE OF 1924

Words and Music by
IRVING BERLIN

Moderate Waltz

What -'ll I do _____ when you _____ are far _____ a -
do _____ when I _____ am won - d'ring

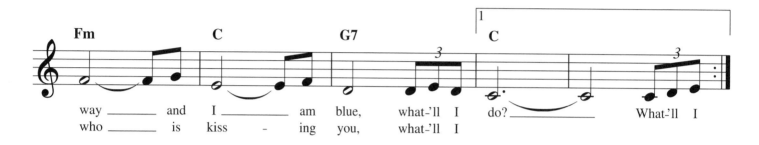

way _____ and I _____ am blue, what-'ll I do? _____ What-'ll I
who _____ is kiss - ing you, what-'ll I

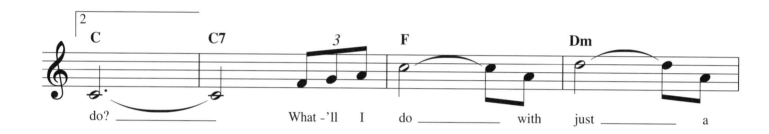

do? _____ What -'ll I do _____ with just _____ a

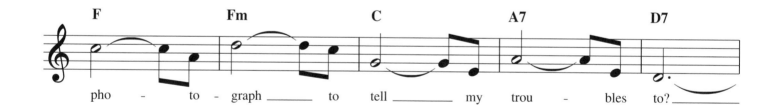

pho - to - graph _____ to tell _____ my trou - bles to? _____

_____ When I'm a - lone _____ with on - ly dreams _____ of

you _____ that won't _____ come true, what-'ll I do? _____

WHEN MY SUGAR WALKS DOWN THE STREET

Words and Music by JIMMIE McHUGH,
GENE AUSTIN and IRVING MILLS

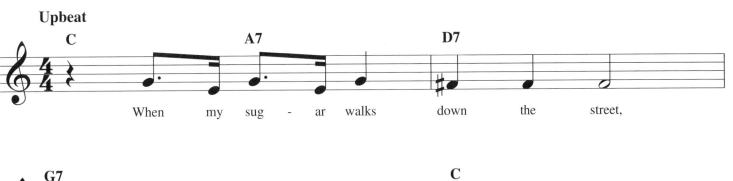

When my sug - ar walks down the street,

all the lit - tle bird - ies go tweet, tweet, tweet.

And in the ev - 'ning when the sun goes down, ___

it's nev - er dark when she's a - round. ___

She's so af - fec - tion - ate and I'll say this, that

when she kiss - es me I sure stay kissed. When my sug - ar walks

down the street, the lit - tle bird - ies go tweet, tweet, tweet.

WHEN THE RED, RED ROBIN COMES BOB, BOB BOBBIN' ALONG
from I'LL CRY TOMORROW

Words and Music by
HARRY WOODS

WHEN YOU'RE SMILING
(The Whole World Smiles with You)

Words and Music by MARK FISHER,
JOE GOODWIN and LARRY SHAY

WHO?
from SUNNY

Lyrics by OTTO HARBACH and OSCAR HAMMERSTEIN
Music by JEROME KER

Brightly

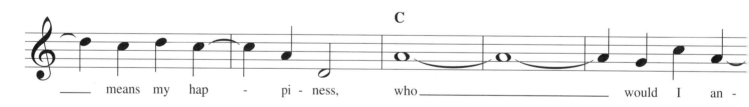

WHO'S SORRY NOW

from THREE LITTLE WORDS

Words by BERT KALMAR and HARRY RUBY
Music by TED SNYDER

WHY DO I LOVE YOU?
from SHOW BOAT

Lyrics by OSCAR HAMMERSTEIN II
Music by JEROME KERN

WITH A SONG IN MY HEART

from SPRING IS HERE

Words by LORENZ HART
Music by RICHARD RODGERS

WITHOUT A SONG

Words by WILLIAM ROSE and EDWARD ELISCU
Music by VINCENT YOUMANS

YES SIR, THAT'S MY BABY

Lyrics by GUS KAHN
Music by WALTER DONALDSON

YES! WE HAVE NO BANANAS

By FRANK SILVER
and IRVING CONN

YOU TOOK ADVANTAGE OF ME
from PRESENT ARMS

Words by LORENZ HART
Music by RICHARD RODGERS

YOU'RE THE CREAM IN MY COFFEE
from HOLD EVERYTHING

Words and Music by B.G. DeSYLVA,
LEW BROWN and RAY HENDERSON

Moderately

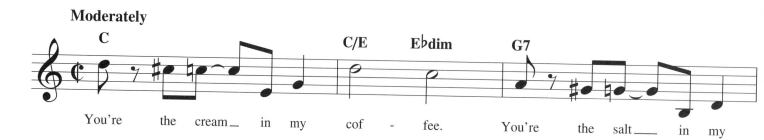

You're   the   cream__   in   my   cof - fee.   You're   the   salt__   in   my

stew.   You   will   al - ways   be   my   ne - ces - si - ty,

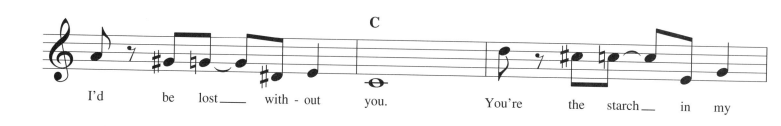

I'd   be   lost__   with - out   you.   You're   the   starch__   in   my

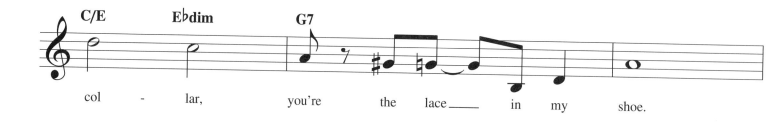

col - lar,   you're   the   lace__   in   my   shoe.

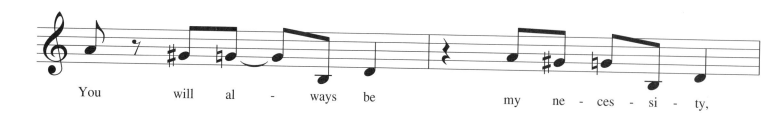

You   will   al - ways   be   my   ne - ces - si - ty,

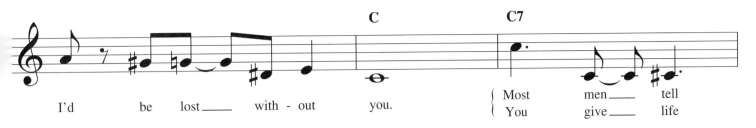

I'd be lost___ with - out you.
{ Most men___ tell
You give___ life

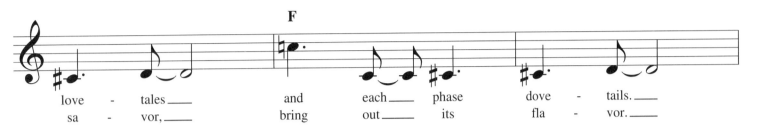

love - tales___ and each___ phase dove - tails.___
sa - vor,___ bring out___ its fla - vor.___

You've heard___ each known way, this way___ is___
So this___ is known clear, dear, you're my___ Wor -

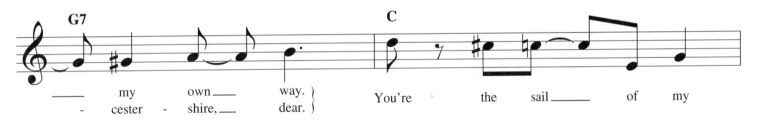

___ my own___ way. } You're the sail___ of my
- cester - shire,___ dear. }

love - boat you're the cap - tain and crew.

You will al - ways be my ne - ces - si - ty

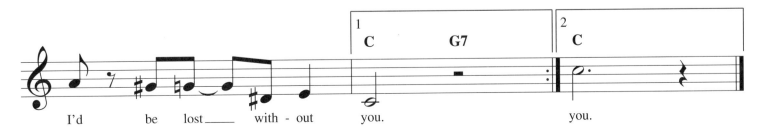

I'd be lost___ with - out you.
you.

CHORD SPELLER

C chords

C	C–E–G
Cm	C–E♭–G
C7	C–E–G–B♭
Cdim	C–E♭–G♭
C+	C–E–G♯

C♯ or D♭ chords

C♯	C♯–F–G♯
C♯m	C♯–E–G♯
C♯7	C♯–F– G♯–B
C♯dim	C♯–E–G
C♯+	C♯–F–A

D chords

D	D–F♯–A
Dm	D–F–A
D7	D–F♯–A–C
Ddim	D–F–A♭
D+	D–F♯–A♯

E♭ chords

E♭	E♭–G–B♭
E♭m	E♭–G♭–B♭
E♭7	E♭–G–B♭–D♭
E♭dim	E♭–G♭–A
E♭+	E♭–G–B

E chords

E	E–G♯–B
Em	E–G–B
E7	E–G♯–B–D
Edim	E–G–B♭
E+	E–G♯–C

F chords

F	F–A–C
Fm	F–A♭–C
F7	F–A–C–E♭
Fdim	F–A♭–B
F+	F–A–C♯

F♯ or G♭ chords

F♯	F♯–A♯–C♯
F♯m	F♯–A–C♯
F♯7	F♯–A♯–C♯–E
F♯dim	F♯–A–C
F♯+	F♯–A♯–D

G chords

G	G–B–D
Gm	G–B♭–D
G7	G–B–D–F
Gdim	G–B♭–D♭
G+	G–B–D♯

G♯ or A♭ chords

A♭	A♭–C–E♭
A♭m	A♭–B–E♭
A♭7	A♭–C–E♭–G♭
A♭dim	A♭–B–D
A♭+	A♭–C–E

A chords

A	A–C♯–E
Am	A–C–E
A7	A–C♯–E–G
Adim	A–C–E♭
A+	A–C♯–F

B♭ chords

B♭	B♭–D–F
B♭m	B♭–D♭–F
B♭7	B♭–D–F–A♭
B♭dim	B♭–D♭–E
B♭+	B♭–D–F♯

B chords

B	B–D♯–F♯
Bm	B–D–F♯
B7	B–D♯–F♯–A
Bdim	B–D–F
B+	B–D♯–G

Important Note: A slash chord (C/E, G/B) tells you that a certain bass note is to be played under a particular harmony. In the case of C/E, the chord is C and the bass note is E.

THE DECADE SERIES

The Decade Series explores the music of the 1890s to the 1990s through each era's major events and personalities. Each volume features text and photos and over 40 of the decade's top songs, showing how music has acted as a mirror or a catalyst for current events and trends. All books are arranged for piano, voice and guitar.

Songs of the 1890s
55 songs: Hello! Ma Baby • Maple Leaf Rag • My Wild Irish Rose • The Sidewalks of New York • Stars and Stripes Forever • When You Were Sweet Sixteen • and more.
00311655...$12.95

Songs of the 1900s (1900-1909)
57 favorites: By the Light of the Silvery Moon • Give My Regards to Broadway • Glow Worm • Meet Me in St. Louis • Take Me Out to the Ball Game • and more.
00311656...$12.95

Songs of the 1910s
57 classics: After You've Gone • Danny Boy • Let Me Call You Sweetheart • My Melancholy Baby • Oh, You Beautiful Doll • When Irish Eyes Are Smiling • and more.
00311657...$12.95

Songs of the '20s
59 songs: Ain't Misbehavin' • April Showers • Baby Face • California Here I Come • Five Foot Two, Eyes of Blue • Manhattan • The Varsity Drag • Who's Sorry Now • more.
00361122...$15.95

Songs of the '30s
62 standards: All of Me • In the Mood • The Lady Is a Tramp • Love Letters in the Sand • My Funny Valentine • Smoke Gets in Your Eyes • What a Diff'rence a Day Made • more.
00361123...$15.95

Songs of the '40s
62 classics: God Bless the Child • How High the Moon • The Last Time I Saw Paris • A Nightingale Sang in Berkeley Square • Swinging On a Star • Tuxedo Junction • more.
00361124 ....$17.95

Songs of the '50s - 2nd Edition
62 songs: Blue Suede Shoes • Blue Velvet • Here's That Rainy Day • Love Me Tender • Misty • Rock Around the Clock • Satin Doll • Tammy • Young at Heart • and more.
00361125...$16.95

Songs of the '60s - 2nd Edition
62 tunes: By the Time I Get to Phoenix • California Dreamin' • Can't Help Falling in Love • Happy Together • I Want to Hold Your Hand • Strangers in the Night • and more.
00361126 ....$16.95

Songs of the '70s
More than 45 songs: Feelings • How Deep Is Your Love • Imagine • Let It Be • Me and Bobby McGee • Piano Man • Send in the Clowns • You Don't Bring Me Flowers • more.
00361127 ....$16.95

Songs of the '80s
Over 40 hits: Candle in the Wind • Ebony and Ivory • Every Breath You Take • Flashdance...What a Feeling • Islands in the Stream • What's Love Got to Do with It • and more.
00490275 ....$16.95

Songs of the '90s
39 great songs: Achy Breaky Heart • Beautiful in My Eyes • Friends in Low Places • Here and Now • Losing My Religion • Save the Best for Last • Tears in Heaven • and more.
00310151 ....$16.95

Songs of the 2000s
35 tunes: Beautiful • Breakaway • Complicated • Don't Know Why • The Space Between • Underneath It All • White Flag • You Raise Me Up • and more.
00311340 ....$16.95

MORE SONGS OF THE DECADE

More Songs of the '20s
Over 50 songs: Ain't We Got Fun? • Fascinating Rhythm • Malagueña • Nobody Knows You When You're Down and Out • Someone to Watch Over Me • and more.
00311647...$15.99

More Songs of the '30s - 2nd Edition
Over 50 favorites: All the Things You Are • A Fine Romance • In a Sentimental Mood • Stompin' at the Savoy • Stormy Weather • Thanks for the Memory • and more.
00311648...$15.99

More Songs of the '40s
60 songs: Bali Ha'i • Be Careful, It's My Heart • San Antonio Rose • Some Enchanted Evening • Too Darn Hot • and more.
00311649 ....$15.95

More Songs of the '50s - 2nd Edition
Over 50 songs: Charlie Brown • Hey, Good Lookin' • Hound Dog • Mona Lisa • (Let Me Be Your) Teddy Bear • That's Amoré • and more.
00311650 ....$15.95

More Songs of the '60s - 2nd Edition
Over 60 songs: Alfie • Born to Be Wild • Moon River • Raindrops Keep Fallin' On My Head • Sweet Caroline • What the World Needs Now • Wooly Bully • and more.
00311651 ....$15.95

More Songs of the '70s
Over 50 songs: Afternoon Delight • All By Myself • American Pie • Happy Days • She Believes in Me • She's Always a Woman • Wishing You Were Here • and more.
00311652 ....$15.95

More Songs of the '80s
43 songs: Addicted to Love • Footloose • Girls Just Want to Have Fun • The Heat Is On • Karma Chameleon • Take My Breath Away • and more.
00311653...$15.95

More Songs of the '90s
Over 30 hits: Blue • Butterfly Kisses • Change the World • Give Me One Reason • I Don't Want to Wait • My Father's Eyes • My Heart Will Go On • more.
00310430 ....$15.95

EVEN MORE SONGS OF THE DECADE

Even More Songs of the '40s
Over 50 classics: Easy Street • It Could Happen to You • Sioux City Sue • Steppin' Out with My Baby • and more.
00311194..$14.95

Even More Songs of the '50s - 2nd Edition
Over 60 great songs: Dream Lover • Great Balls of Fire • La Bamba • Love and Marriage • Wake Up Little Susie • more.
00310986..$14.95

Even More Songs of the '60s
59 super hits: Daydream Believer • Good Vibrations • My Girl • Respect • Twist and Shout • Yesterday • and more.
00310987..$14.95

Even More Songs of the '70s
51 top songs: I Honestly Love You • I'll Be There • Joy to the World • Time in a Bottle • Y.M.C.A. • and more.
00310988..$14.95

Even More Songs of the '80s
39 hits: Chariots of Fire • Jack and Diane • Lady in Red • Missing You • Thriller • Walk Like an Egyptian • more.
00311031 ....$14.95

STILL MORE SONGS OF THE DECADE

Still More Songs of the '30s - 2nd Edition
Over 50 songs: April in Paris • Heat Wave • It Don't Mean a Thing (If It Ain't Got That Swing) • and more.
00310027......................................$15.95

Still More Songs of the '40s
Over 50 favorites: Don't Get Around Much Anymore • If I Loved You • Sentimental Journey • and more.
00310028......................................$15.95

Still More Songs of the '50s - 2nd Edition
Over 50 classics: Autumn Leaves • Chantilly Lace • If I Were a Bell • Luck Be a Lady • Venus • and more.
00310029......................................$15.95

Still More Songs of the '60s
Over 50 songs: Duke of Earl • I'm Henry VIII, I Am • Leader of the Pack • What a Wonderful World • and more.
00311680......................................$15.95

Still More Songs of the '70s
54 hits: Cat's in the Cradle • Nadia's Theme • The Way We Were • You've Got a Friend • and more.
00311683......................................$15.95

Still More Songs of the '80s
40 songs: All I Need • Jessie's Girl • Sweet Dreams (Are Made of This) • Up Where We Belong • and more.
00310321 ....$15.95

Still More Songs of the '90s
40 hits: Fields of Gold • From a Distance • Jump Jive An' Wail • Kiss Me • Mambo No. 5 • and more.
00310575......................................$15.95

FOR MORE INFORMATION,
SEE YOUR LOCAL MUSIC DEALER,
OR WRITE TO:

HAL•LEONARD®
CORPORATION
7777 W. BLUEMOUND RD. P.O. BOX 13819
MILWAUKEE, WISCONSIN 53213

Prices, contents, and availability subject to change without notice
Complete contents listings available online at **www.halleonard.com.**

THE ULTIMATE COLLECTION OF
FAKE BOOKS

The Real Book – Sixth Edition

Hal Leonard proudly presents the first legitimate and legal editions of these books ever produced. These bestselling titles are mandatory for anyone who plays jazz! Over 400 songs, including: All By Myself • Dream a Little Dream of Me • God Bless the Child • Like Someone in Love • When I Fall in Love • and more.

00240221	Volume 1, C Edition	$29.95
00240224	Volume 1, B♭ Edition	$29.95
00240225	Volume 1, E♭ Edition	$29.95
00240226	Volume 1, BC Edition	$29.95
00240222	Volume 2, C Edition	$29.95
00240227	Volume 2, B♭ Edition	$29.95
00240228	Volume 2, E♭ Edition	$29.95

Best Fake Book Ever – 3rd Edition

More than 1,000 songs from all styles of music, including: All My Loving • At the Hop • Cabaret • Dust in the Wind • Fever • From a Distance • Hello, Dolly! • Hey Jude • King of the Road • Longer • Misty • Route 66 • Sentimental Journey • Somebody • Song Sung Blue • Spinning Wheel • Unchained Melody • We Will Rock You • What a Wonderful World • Wooly Bully • Y.M.C.A. • and more.

00290239	C Edition	$49.95
00240083	B♭ Edition	$49.95
00240084	E♭ Edition	$49.95

Classic Rock Fake Book – 2nd Edition

This fake book is a great compilation of more than 250 terrific songs of the rock era, arranged for piano, voice, guitar and all C instruments. Includes: All Right Now • American Woman • Birthday • Honesty • I Shot the Sheriff • I Want You to Want Me • Imagine • It's Still Rock and Roll to Me • Lay Down Sally • Layla • My Generation • Rock and Roll All Nite • Spinning Wheel • White Room • We Will Rock You • lots more!

00240108 $29.95

Classical Fake Book – 2nd Edition

This unprecedented, amazingly comprehensive reference includes over 850 classical themes and melodies for all classical music lovers. Includes everything from Renaissance music to Vivaldi and Mozart to Mendelssohn. Lyrics in the original language are included when appropriate.

00240044 $34.95

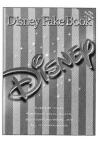

The Disney Fake Book – 2nd Edition

Over 200 of the most beloved songs of all time, including: Be Our Guest • Can You Feel the Love Tonight • Colors of the Wind • Cruella De Vil • Friend Like Me • Heigh-Ho • It's a Small World • Mickey Mouse March • Supercalifragilisticexpialidocious • Under the Sea • When You Wish upon a Star • A Whole New World • Zip-A-Dee-Doo-Dah • and more!

00240039 $27.95

The Folksong Fake Book

Over 1,000 folksongs perfect for performers, school teachers, and hobbyists. Includes: Bury Me Not on the Lone Prairie • Clementine • Danny Boy • The Erie Canal • Go, Tell It on the Mountain • Home on the Range • Kumbaya • Michael Row the Boat Ashore • Shenandoah • Simple Gifts • Swing Low, Sweet Chariot • When Johnny Comes Marching Home • Yankee Doodle • and many more.

00240151 $24.95

The Hymn Fake Book

Nearly 1,000 multi-denominational hymns perfect for church musicians or hobbyists: Amazing Grace • Christ the Lord Is Risen Today • For the Beauty of the Earth • It Is Well with My Soul • A Mighty Fortress Is Our God • O for a Thousand Tongues to Sing • Praise to the Lord, the Almighty • Take My Life and Let It Be • What a Friend We Have in Jesus • and hundreds more!

00240145 $24.95

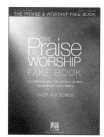

The Praise & Worship Fake Book

400 songs: As the Deer • Better Is One Day • Come, Now Is the Time to Worship • Firm Foundation • Glorify Thy Name • Here I Am to Worship • I Could Sing of Your Love Forever • Lord, I Lift Your Name on High • More Precious Than Silver • Open the Eyes of My Heart • The Power of Your Love • Shine, Jesus, Shine • Trading My Sorrows • We Fall Down • You Are My All in All • and more.

00240234 $34.95

The R&B Fake Book – 2nd Edition

This terrific fake book features 375 classic R&B hits: Baby Love • Best of My Love • Dancing in the Street • Easy • Get Ready • Heatwave • Here and Now • Just Once • Let's Get It On • The Loco-Motion • (You Make Me Feel Like) A Natural Woman • One Sweet Day • Papa Was a Rollin' Stone • Save the Best for Last • September • Sexual Healing • Shop Around • Still • Tell It Like It Is • Up on the Roof • Walk on By • What's Going On • more!

00240107   C Edition $29.95

Ultimate Broadway Fake Book – 4th Edition

More than 700 show-stoppers from over 200 shows! Includes: Ain't Misbehavin' • All I Ask of You • Bewitched • Camelot • Don't Cry for Me Argentina • Edelweiss • I Dreamed a Dream • If I Were a Rich Man • Memory • Oklahoma • Send in the Clowns • What I Did for Love • more.

00240046 $47.50

FOR MORE INFORMATION, SEE YOUR LOCAL MUSIC DEALER, OR WRITE TO:

HAL•LEONARD® CORPORATION
7777 W. BLUEMOUND RD. P.O. BOX 13819 MILWAUKEE. WI 53213

Complete songlists available online at
www.halleonard.com

Prices, contents and availabilty subject to change without notice.

The Ultimate Christmas Fake Book – 5th Edition

This updated edition includes 2[?] traditional and contemporary Christmas songs: Away in a Manger • The Christmas Song • Deck the Hall • Frosty the Snow Man • A Holly Jolly Christmas • I Heard the Bells on Christmas Day • Jingle Bells • Little Saint Nick • Merry Christmas, Darling • Nuttin' for Christmas • Rudolph the Red-Nosed Reindeer • Silent Night • What Child Is This? • more.

00240045 $24.95

The Ultimate Country Fake Book – 5th Edition

This book includes over 700 of your favorite country hits: Always on My Mind • Boot Scootin' Boogie • Crazy • Down at the Twist and Shout • Forever and Ever, Amen • Friends in Low Places • The Gambler • Jambalaya • King of the Road • Sixteen Tons • There's a Tear in My Beer • Your Cheatin' Heart • and hundreds more.

00240049 $39.95

The Ultimate Fake Book – 4th Edition

Includes over 1,200 hits: Blue Skies • Body and Soul • Endless Love • Foggy Day • Isn't It Romantic? • Memory • Mona Lisa • Moon River • Operator • Piano Man • Roxanne • Satin Doll • Shout • Small World • Speak Softly, Love • Strawberry Fields Forever • Tears in Heaven • Unforgettable • hundreds more!

00240024	C Edition	$49.95
00240026	B♭ Edition	$49.95
00240025	E♭ Edition	$49.95

The Ultimate Pop/Rock Fake Book – 4th Edition

Over 600 pop standards and contemporary hits, including: All Shook Up • Another One Bites the Dust • Crying • Don't Know Much • Dust in the Wind • Earth Angel • Every Breath You Take • Hero • Hey Jude • Hold My Hand • Imagine • Layla • The Loco-Motion • Oh, Pretty Woman • On Broadway • Spinning Wheel • Stand by Me • Stayin' Alive • Tears in Heaven • True Colors • The Twist • Vision of Love • A Whole New World • Wild Thing • Wooly Bully • Yesterday • more!

00240099 $39.95

Fake Book of the World's Favorite Songs – 4th Edition

Over 700 favorites, including: America the Beautiful • Anchors Aweigh • Battle Hymn of the Republic • Bill Bailey, Won't You Please Come Home • Chopsticks • Für Elise • His Eye Is on the Sparrow • I Wonder Who's Kissing Her Now • Jesu, Joy of Man's Desiring • My Old Kentucky Home • Sidewalks of New York • Take Me Out to the Ball Game • When the Saints Go Marching In • and hundreds more!

00240072 $22.95

0409

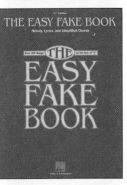

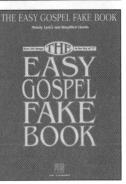

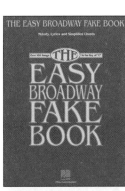

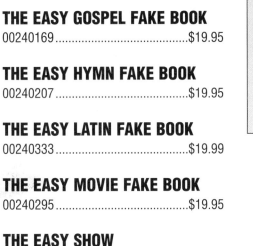